Handbook of Exorcism

Compiled by
Lester Bivens

Scribbles

Year of Publication 2018

ISBN : 9789352979578

Book Published by

Scribbles

(An Imprint of Alpha Editions)

email - alphaedis@gmail.com

Produced by: PediaPress GmbH
Limburg an der Lahn
Germany
http://pediapress.com/

The content within this book was generated collaboratively by volunteers. Please be advised that nothing found here has necessarily been reviewed by people with the expertise required to provide you with complete, accurate or reliable information. Some information in this book may be misleading or simply wrong. Alpha Editions and PediaPress does not guarantee the validity of the information found here. If you need specific advice (for example, medical, legal, financial, or risk management) please seek a professional who is licensed or knowledgeable in that area.

Sources, licenses and contributors of the articles and images are listed in the section entitled "References". Parts of the books may be licensed under the GNU Free Documentation License. A copy of this license is included in the section entitled "GNU Free Documentation License"

The views and characters expressed in the book are those of the contributors and his/her imagination and do not represent the views of the Publisher.

Contents

Articles   1

Introduction   1
    Exorcism 1

In Christianity   13
    Exorcism in Christianity 13
    Minor exorcism in Christianity 27
    Exorcism in the Catholic Church 31

In Islam   39
    Exorcism in Islam 39

In Buddhism   45
    Ghosts in Tibetan culture 45

Notable exorcisms and exorcists   49
    Louviers possessions 49
    Aix-en-Provence possessions 52
    Loudun possessions 56
    Anneliese Michel 64
    Martha Brossier 71

Appendix **73**

References 73

Article Sources and Contributors 77

Image Sources, Licenses and Contributors 78

Article Licenses **79**

Index **81**

Introduction

Exorcism

Part of a series on the
Paranormal

Painting of Saint Francis Borgia performing an exorcism, by Goya

- v
- t
- e[1]

Exorcism (from Greek εξορκισμός, *exorkismós* "binding by oath") is the religious or spiritual practice of evicting demons or other spiritual entities from a person, or an area, that are believed to be possessed. Depending on the spiritual beliefs of the exorcist, this may be done by causing the entity to swear an oath, performing an elaborate ritual, or simply by commanding it to depart

Figure 1: *Christ Exorcising a Mute by Gustav Dore, 1865.*

in the name of a higher power. The practice is ancient and part of the belief system of many cultures and religions.

Requested and performed exorcism began to decline in the United States by the 18th century and occurred rarely until the latter half of the 20th century when the public saw a sharp rise due to the media attention exorcisms were getting. There was "a 50% increase in the number of exorcisms performed between the early 1960s and the mid-1970s".

Christianity

In Christianity, exorcism is the practice of casting out demons. In Christian practice the person performing the exorcism, known as an exorcist, is often a member of the Christian Church, or an individual thought to be graced with special powers or skills. The exorcist may use prayers and religious material, such as set formulas, gestures, symbols, icons, amulets, etc. The exorcist often invokes God, Jesus and/or several different angels and archangels to intervene with the exorcism. Protestant Christian exorcists most commonly believe the authority given to them by the Father, Son, and Holy Spirit (the Trinity) is the source of their ability to cast out demons.[2]

Figure 2: *The statue of Saint Philip of Agira with the Gospel in his left hand, the symbol of the exorcists, in the May celebrations in his honor at Limina, Sicily*

In general, people considered to be possessed are not regarded as evil in themselves, nor wholly responsible for their actions, because possession is considered to be unwilling manipulation by a demon resulting in harm to self or others. Therefore, practitioners regard exorcism as more of a cure than a punishment. The mainstream rituals usually take this into account, making sure that there is no violence to the possessed, only that they be tied down if there is potential for violence.[3]

Catholic Church

In Catholic Christianity, exorcisms are performed in the name of Jesus Christ. A distinction is made between a formal exorcism, which can only be conducted by a priest during a baptism or with the permission of a bishop, and "prayers of deliverance" which can be said by anyone.

The Catholic rite for a formal exorcism, called a "Major Exorcism", is given in Section 11 of the Rituale Romanum. The Ritual lists guidelines for conducting an exorcism, and for determining when a formal exorcism is required. Priests are instructed to carefully determine that the nature of the affliction is not actually a psychological or physical illness before proceeding.

In Catholic practice the person performing the exorcism, known as an exorcist, is an ordained priest. The exorcist recites prayers according to the rubrics of the

Figure 3: *The image of Hanuman at the Hanuman temple in Sarangpur is said to be so powerful that a mere look at it by people affected by evil spirits, drives the evil spirits out of the people affected*

rite, and may make use of religious materials such as icons and sacramentals. The exorcist invokes God—specifically the Name of Jesus—as well as members of the Church Triumphant and the Archangel Michael to intervene with the exorcism. According to Catholic understanding, several weekly exorcisms over many years are sometimes required to expel a deeply entrenched demon.

Lutheran Churches

From the 16th century onward, Lutheran pastoral handbooks describe the primary symptoms of demonic possession to be knowledge of secret things, knowledge of languages one has never learned, and supernatural strength. Before conducting a major exorcism, Lutheran liturgical texts state that a physician be consulted in order to rule out any medical or psychiatric illness. The rite of exorcism centers chiefly around driving out demons "with prayers and contempt" and includes the Apostle's Creed and Our Father.

Baptismal liturgies in Lutheran Churches include a minor exorcism.

Hinduism

Beliefs and practices pertaining to the practice of exorcism are prominently connected with Hindus. Of the four Vedas (holy books of the Hindus), the Atharva Veda is said to contain the secrets related to exorcism, magic and alchemy. The basic means of exorcism are the *mantra* and the *yajna* used in both Vedic and Tantric traditions. Vaishnava traditions also employ a recitation of names of Narasimha and reading scriptures, notably the *Bhagavata Purana* aloud.

According to Gita Mahatmya of Padma Purana, reading the 3rd, 7th and 9th chapter of Bhagavad Gita and mentally offering the result to departed persons helps them to get released from their ghostly situation. *Kirtan*, continuous playing of mantras, keeping scriptures and holy pictures of the deities (Shiva, Vishnu, Hanuman, Brahma, Shakti, etc.) (especially of Narasimha) in the house, burning incense offered during a *Puja*, sprinkling water from holy rivers, and blowing conches used in *puja* are other effective practices.Wikipedia:Citation needed It is also believed that praying to Lord Hanuman gives the best result. It is also mentioned in the Hanuman Chalisa. It is believed that just uttering the name of Lord Hanuman makes the evil forces and devils tremble, in fear.

The main puranic resource on ghost and death-related information is Garuda Purana.

A complete description of birth and death and also about the human soul are explained in Katō Upanishad, a part of Yajur Veda. A summary of this is also available as a separate scripture called Kāttakaṃ.

Islam

In Islam, exorcism is called *ruqya*. It is used to repair the damage caused by *sihr* or black magic. Exorcisms today are part of a wider body of contemporary Islamic alternative medicine called *al-Tibb al-Nabawi* (Medicine of the Prophet).

Islamic exorcisms consist of the treated person lying down, while a sheikh places a hand on a patient's head while reciting verses from the Quran, but this is not mandatory. The drinking or sprinkling of holy water (water from the Zamzam Well) may also take place along with applying of clean non-alcohol-based perfumes, called as ittar.

Specific verses from the Quran are recited, which glorify God (e.g. The Throne Verse (Arabic: آية الكرسي *Ayatul Kursi*)), and invoke God's help. In some cases, the *adhan* (call for daily prayers) is also read, as this has the effect of repelling non-angelic unseen beings or the *jinn*.Wikipedia:Citation needed

The Islamic prophet Muhammad taught his followers to read the last three *suras* from the Quran, Surat al-Ikhlas (The Fidelity), Surat al-Falaq (The Dawn) and Surat an-Nas (Mankind).Wikipedia:Citation needed

A *hadith* recorded in *Sahih al-Bukhari*, 8:76:479[4] states: "Seventy thousand people of my followers will enter Paradise without accounts, and they are those who do not practice Ar-Ruqya and do not see an evil omen in things, and put their trust in their Lord." Ibn Qayyim al-Jawziyya, a scholar, commented on this *hadith*, stating: That is because these people will enter Paradise without being called to account because of the perfection of their Tawheed, therefore he described them as people who did not ask others to perform ruqyah for them. Hence he said "and they put their trust in their Lord." Because of their complete trust in their Lord, their contentment with Him, their faith in Him, their being pleased with Him and their seeking their needs from Him, they do not ask people for anything, be it ruqyah or anything else, and they are not influenced by omens and superstitions that could prevent them from doing what they want to do, because superstition detracts from and weakens Tawheed".

Judaism

Josephus reports exorcisms performed by administering poisonous root extracts and others by making sacrifices.[5]

In more recent times, Rabbi Yehuda Fetaya (1859-1942) authored the book *Minchat Yahuda*, which deals extensively with exorcism, his experience with possessed people, and other subjects of Jewish thought. The book is written in Hebrew and was translated into English.

The Jewish exorcism ritual is performed by a rabbi who has mastered practical Kabbalah. Also present is a minyan (a group of ten adult males), who gather in a circle around the possessed person. The group recites Psalm 91 three times, and then the rabbi blows a shofar (a ram's horn).

The shofar is blown in a certain way, with various notes and tones, in effect to "shatter the body" so that the possessing force will be shaken loose. After it has been shaken loose, the rabbi begins to communicate with it and ask it questions such as why it is possessing the body of the possessed. The minyan may pray for it and perform a ceremony for it in order to enable it to feel safe, and so that it can leave the person's body.

Taoism

In Taoism, exorcisms are performed because an individual has been possessed by an evil spirit for one of two reasons. The individual has disturbed a ghost, regardless of intent, and the ghost now seeks revenge. An alive person could also be jealous and uses black magic as revenge thereby conjuring a ghost to possess someone.[6] Members of the fashi, both Chinese ritual officers and priests ordained by a celestial master, perform Chinese rituals, in particular, exorcisms.

Historically, Taoist exorcisms include chanting, physical movements, and praying as a way to drive away the spirit.[7] Rituals such as these occur during festivals. Rituals such as these are considered of low order during these festivals. They are more for entertainment than a necessity during festivals.

The leaders of the exorcisms create a dramatic performance to call out the demons so the village can once again have peace. The leaders strike themselves with a sharp weapon so they bleed. Blood is considered to be a protector, so after the rituals, the blood is blotted with a tissue and put on the door of houses as an act of protection against evil spirits.[8]

Buddhism

The ritual of the Exorcising-Ghost day is part of Tibetan tradition. The Tibetan religious ceremony 'Gutor' ༼དགུ་གཏོར་༽, literally offering of the 29th, is held on the 29th of the 12th Tibetan month, with its focus on driving out all negativity, including evil spirits and misfortunes of the past year, and starting the new year in a peaceful and auspicious way.

The temples and monasteries throughout Tibet hold grand religious dance ceremonies, with the largest at Potala Palace in Lhasa. Families clean their houses on this day, decorate the rooms and eat a special noodle soup called 'Guthuk'. ༼དགུ་ཐུག༽ In the evening, the people carry torches, calling out the words of exorcism.

Scientific view

Demonic possession is not a psychiatric or medical diagnosis recognized by either the DSM-5 or the ICD-10. Those who profess a belief in demonic possession have sometimes ascribed to possession the symptoms associated with physical or mental illnesses, such as hysteria, mania, psychosis, Tourette's syndrome, epilepsy, schizophrenia or dissociative identity disorder.[9,10,11,12,13,14]

Additionally, there is a form of monomania called demonomania or demonopathy in which the patient believes that he or she is possessed by one or more demons.[15] The illusion that exorcism works on people experiencing symptoms of possession is attributed by some to placebo effect and the power of suggestion.[16,17] Some cases suggest that supposedly possessed persons are actually narcissists or are suffering from low self-esteem and act demonically possessed in order to gain attention.[18]

Within the scientific community, the work of psychiatrist M. Scott Peck, a believer in exorcism, generated significant debate and derision. Much was made of his association with (and admiration for) the controversial Malachi Martin, a Roman Catholic priest and a former Jesuit, despite the fact that Peck consistently called Martin a liar and a manipulator.[19] Other criticisms leveled against Peck included claims that he had transgressed the boundaries of professional ethics by attempting to persuade his patients to accept Christianity.[20]

Exorcism and mental illness

One scholar has described psychosurgery as "Neurosurgical Exorcisms", with trepanation having been widely used to release demons from the brain.[21] Meanwhile, another scholar has equated psychotherapy with exorcism.[22]

United Kingdom

In the UK, exorcisms are increasing. They happen mainly in charismatic and Pentecostal churches, and also among communities of West African origin. Frequently, the people exorcised are mentally disturbed. Mentally ill people are sometimes told to stop their medication as the church believes prayer and/or exorcism is enough. If psychiatric patients do not get better after exorcism, they may believe they have failed to overcome the demon and get worse.[23]

Notable exorcisms and exorcists

- (1578) Martha Broissier was a young woman who was made famous around the year of 1578 for her feigned demonic possession discovered through exorcism proceedings.
- (1619) Mademoiselle Elizabeth de Ranfaing, who having become a widow in 1617 was later sought in marriage by a physician (afterwards burned under judicial sentence for being a practicing magician). After being rejected, he gave her philters to make her love him which occasioned strange developments in her health and proceeded to continuously give her some other forms of medicament. The maladies which she suffered were incurable by the various physicians that attended her and eventually

lead to a recourse of exorcisms as prescribed by several physicians that examined her case. They began to exorcise her in September, 1619. During the exorcisms, the demon that possessed her made detailed and fluid responses in varying languages including French, Greek, Latin, Hebrew and Italian and was reportedly able to know and recite the thoughts and sins of various individuals who examined her. She was further also able to describe in detail with the use of various languages the rites and secrets of the church to experts in the languages she spoke. There was even a mention of how the demon interrupted an exorcist, who after making a mistake in his recital of an exorcism rite in Latin, corrected his speech and mocked him.

- (1778) George Lukins
- (1842-1844) Johann Blumhardt performed the exorcism of Gottliebin Dittus over a two-year period in Möttlingen, Germany from 1842–1844. Pastor Blumhardt's parish subsequently experienced growth marked by confession and healing, which he attributed to the successful exorcism.
- (1906) Clara Germana Cele was a South African school girl who claimed to be possessed.
- (1947) Salvador Dalí is reputed to have received an exorcism from Italian friar Gabriele Maria Berardi while he was in France. Dalí created a sculpture of Christ on the cross that he gave the friar in thanks.[24]
- (1949) A boy identified as Robbie Mannheim, was the subject of an exorcism in 1949, which became the chief inspiration for *The Exorcist*, a horror novel and film written by William Peter Blatty, who heard about the case while he was a student in the class of 1950 at Georgetown University. Robbie was taken into the care of Rev. Luther Miles Schulze, the boy's Lutheran pastor, after psychiatric and medical doctors were unable to explain the disturbing events associated with the teen; the minister then referred the boy to Rev. Edward Hughes, who performed the first exorcism on the teen. The subsequent exorcism was partially performed in both Cottage City, Maryland and Bel-Nor, Missouri by Father William S. Bowdern, S.J., Father Raymond Bishop S.J. and a then Jesuit scholastic Fr. Walter Halloran, S.J.
- (1974) Michael Taylor
- (1975) Anneliese Michel was a Catholic woman from Germany who was said to be possessed by six or more demons and subsequently underwent a secret ten-month-long voluntary exorcism. Two motion pictures, *The Exorcism of Emily Rose* and *Requiem*, are loosely based on Anneliese's story. The documentary movie *Exorcism of Anneliese Michel* (in Polish, with English subtitles) features the original audio tapes from the exorcism. The two priests and her parents were convicted of negligent manslaughter for failing to call a medical doctor to address her eating disorder as she

died weighing only 68 pounds. The case has been labelled a misidentification of mental illness, negligence, abuse, and religious hysteria.[25]
- Bobby Jindal, former governor of Louisiana, wrote an essay in 1994 about his personal experience of performing an exorcism on an intimate friend named "Susan" while in college.
- Mother Teresa allegedly underwent an exorcism late in life under the direction of the Archbishop of Calcutta, Henry D'Souza, after he noticed she seemed to be extremely agitated in her sleep and feared she "might be under the attack of the evil one."
- (2005) Tanacu exorcism is a case in which a mentally ill Romanian nun was killed during an exorcism by priest Daniel Petre Corogeanu.
- The October 2007 mākutu lifting in the Wellington, New Zealand suburb of Wainuiomata led to a death by drowning of a woman and the hospitalization of a teen. After a long trial, five family members were convicted and sentenced to non-custodial sentences.

References

Works cited

- Monier-Williams, Monier (1974), *Brahmanism and Hinduism: Or, Religious Thought and Life in India, as Based on the Veda and Other Sacred Books of the Hindus*[26], Elibron Classics, Adamant Media Corporation, ISBN 1-4212-6531-1, retrieved 8 July 2007

Further reading

- Abraham Hartwell (1599). *A True Discourse Upon the Matter of Martha Brossier of Romorantin, pretended to be possessed by a Devil. 2018.* ISBN 1987654439.
- Augustin Calmet (1751) "Treatise on the Apparitions of Spirits and on Vampires or Revenants: of Hungary, Moravia, et al. The Complete Volumes I & II. 2016 ISBN 978-1-5331-4568-0
- Barry Beyerstein. (1995). *Dissociative States: Possession and Exorcism.* In Gordon Stein (ed.). *The Encyclopedia of the Paranormal.* Prometheus Books. pp. 544–52. ISBN 1-57392-021-5
- Catechism of the Catholic Church, nn. 391–95; 407.409.414.
- David M. Kiely and Christina McKenna. (2007). *The Dark Sacrament : True Stories of Modern-Day Demon Possession and Exorcism.* HarperOne. ISBN 0-06-123816-3
- Frederick M. Smith. (2006). *The Self Possessed: Deity and Spirit Possession in South Asian Literature and Civilization.* New York: Columbia University Press. ISBN 0-231-13748-6

- Josephine McCarthy. (2010). *The Exorcists Handbook*. Golem Media Publishers. ISBN 978-1-933993-91-1
- Gabriele Amorth. (1999). *An Exorcist Tells His Story*. San Francisco: Ignatius Press.
- Girolamo Menghi, Gaetano Paxia. (2002). *The Devil's Scourge – Exorcism during the Italian Renaissance*. Weiser Books.
- Kazuhiro Tajima-Pozo et al. (2011). "Practicing exorcism in schizophrenia"[27]. Case Reports.
- Michael W. Cuneo, *American Exorcism: Expelling Demons in the Land of Plenty*, Doubleday. 2001. ISBN 0-385-50176-5. Sociological account.
- Malachi Martin. (1976). *Hostage to the Devil: The Possession and Exorcism of Five Living Americans*. ISBN 0-06-065337-X
- M. Scott Peck. (2005). *Glimpses of the Devil: A Psychiatrist's Personal Accounts of Possession, Exorcism, and Redemption*.
- William Trethowan. (1976). "Exorcism: A Psychiatric Viewpoint"[28]. Journal of Medical Ethics 2: 127–37.
- Walter F. Williams. (2000). *Encyclopedia of Pseudoscience: From Alien Abductions to Zone Therapy*. Fitzroy Dearborn. pp. 103–04

External links

- "Exorcism: Facts and Fiction About Demonic Possession"[29] by Benjamin Radford.
- "An Evening with an Exorcist," a talk given by Fr. Thomas J. Euteneuer[30]* Catholic Exorcism – Web Site[31]
- Bobby Jindal. BEATING A DEMON: Physical Dimensions of Spiritual Warfare. (New Oxford Review, December 1994)[32]
- ⓦ Herbermann, Charles, ed. (1913). "Exorcism". *Catholic Encyclopedia*. New York: Robert Appleton Company.
- ⓦ "Exorcism". *Encyclopædia Britannica* (11th ed.). 1911.
- Jewish Encyclopedia: Exorcism[33]
- Diocese of Worcester webpages on Ministry of Deliverance[34] Anglican View
- Exorcism in the Orthodox Church[35]
- The Catholic Prayer of Exorcism in Latin[36]

In Christianity

Exorcism in Christianity

Exorcism in Christianity is the practice of casting out demons from a person they are believed to have possessed. The person performing the exorcism, known as an exorcist, is often a member of the Christian Church, or an individual thought to be graced with special powers or skills. The exorcist may use prayers and religious material, such as set formulas, gestures, symbols, icons, amulets, etc. The exorcist often invokes God, Jesus and/or several different angels and archangels to intervene with the exorcism. A survey of Christian exorcists found that most exorcists believe that any mature Christian can perform an exorcism, not just members of clergy. Christian exorcists most commonly believe the authority given to them by the Father, Son, and Holy Spirit (the Trinity) is the source of their ability to cast out demons.[37]

The term became prominent in Early Christianity from the early 2nd century onward.

In general, people considered to be possessed are not regarded as evil in themselves, nor wholly responsible for their actions, because possession is considered to be unwilling manipulation by a demon resulting in harm to self or others. Therefore, practitioners regard exorcism as more of a cure than a punishment. The mainstream rituals usually take this into account, making sure that there is no violence to the possessed, only that they be tied down if there is potential for violence.[38]

Old Testament

The *Catholic Encyclopedia* says that there is only one apparent case of demonic possession in the Old Testament, of King Saul being tormented by an "evil spirit" (1 Samuel 16:14), but it relies on an interpretation of the Hebrew word "rûah" as "evil spirit", an interpretation that is doubted by the *Catholic*

Figure 4: *Christ Exorcising a Mute by Gustav Dore, 1865.*

Encyclopedia. The *Catholic Encyclopedia* ties exorcism methods mentioned in extra-canonical Jewish literature to the driving off of a demon in the book of Tobias. Some theologians such as Ángel Manuel Rodríguez say that mediums like the ones mentioned in Leviticus 20:27 were possessed by demons.

New Testament

Christian exorcism is founded on the belief that Jesus commanded his followers to expel evil spirits in his name.[39] According to the Catholic Encyclopedia article on Exorcism, Jesus points to this ability as a sign of his Messiahship, and he empowered his disciples to do the same.

The Lutheran Church–Missouri Synod traces the practice of exorcism to the Scriptural claim that Jesus Christ expelled demons with a simple command (Mark 1:23–26; 9:14–29; Luke 11:14–26). The apostles continued the practice with the power and in the name of Jesus (Matthew 10:1; Acts 19:11–16).

The Jewish Encyclopedia article on Jesus states that Jesus, "was devoted especially to casting out demons," and also believed that he passed this on to his followers; however, "his superiority to his followers was shown by his casting out demons which they had failed to expel."[40]

Figure 5: *Painting by Francisco Goya of Saint Francis Borgia performing an exorcism.*

History

Early church

St. Cyril of Jerusalem wrote, "Receive the exorcisms with devotion...Divine exorcisms, borrowed from the Scripture, purify the soul."

Middle Ages

The Benedictine *Vade retro satana* was used in the medieval era.

In the 15th century, Catholic exorcists were both clerical and lay, since every Christian has the power to command demons and drive them out in the name of Christ.

Reformation

After the Protestant Reformation, Martin Luther abbreviated the Roman ritual used for exorcism. In 1526, the ritual was further abbreviated and the exsufflation was omitted. This form of the *Lutheran Ritual for Exorcism* was incorporated into the majority of the Lutheran service-books and implemented.

Current beliefs and practices

Anglicanism

Church of England

In 1974, the Church of England set up the "Deliverance ministry". As part of its creation, every diocese in the country was equipped with a team trained in both exorcism and psychiatry. According to its representatives, most cases brought before it have conventional explanations, and actual exorcisms are quite rare; blessings, though, are sometimes given to people for psychological reasons.

Anglican priests may not perform an exorcism without permission from the Diocesan bishop. An exorcism is not usually performed unless the bishop and his team of specialists (including a psychiatrist and physician) have approved it.

Episcopal Church

In the Episcopal Church, the *Book of Occasional Services* discusses provision for exorcism; but it does not indicate any specific rite, nor does it establish an office of "exorcist".[41] Diocesan exorcists usually continue in their role when they have retired from all other church duties.

Baptists

Albert Mohler, the ninth president of the Southern Baptist Theological Seminary, states that Baptists, among other evangelical Christians, do <templatestyles src="Template:Quote/styles.css"/>

> believe in the existence, malevolence, and power of the Devil and demons. About these things, the New Testament is abundantly clear. We must resist any effort to 'demythologize' the New Testament in order to deny the existence of these evil forces and beings. At the same time, we must recognize quickly that the Devil and demons are not accorded the powers often ascribed to them in popular piety. The Devil is indeed a threat, as Peter made clear when he warned: 'Be sober-minded; be watchful. Your adversary the devil prowls around like a roaring lion, seeking someone to devour.' [1 Peter 5:8] The New Testament is also clear that very real cases of demonic possession were encountered by Jesus and his followers. Jesus liberated afflicted individuals as he commanded the demons to flee, and they obeyed him. Likewise, the Apostle Paul performed exorcisms as he confronted the powers of evil and darkness in his ministry. A closer look at the crucial passages involved reveals no rite of exorcism, however, just the name of Jesus and the proclamation of the Gospel. Likewise,

Figure 6: *The statue of Saint Philip of Agira with the Gospel in his left hand, the symbol of the exorcists, in the May celebrations in his honor at Limina, Sicily*

there is no notion of a priestly ministry of ordained exorcists in the New Testament.

As a result of this theology, for the Baptist Christian, the weapons of "warfare are spiritual, and the powers that the forces of darkness most fear are the name of Jesus, the authority of the Bible, and the power of his Gospel."

Catholicism

In Catholic dogma exorcism is a sacramental but not a sacrament, unlike baptism or confession. Unlike a sacrament, exorcism's "integrity and efficacy do not depend ... on the rigid use of an unchanging formula or on the ordered sequence of prescribed actions. Its efficacy depends on two elements: authorization from valid and licit Church authorities, and the faith of the exorcist."[42]

The Catholic Church revised the Rite of Exorcism in January 1999, though the traditional Rite of Exorcism in Latin is allowed as an option. The act of exorcism is considered to be an incredibly dangerous spiritual task. The ritual assumes that possessed persons retain their free will, though the demon may hold control over their physical body, and involves prayers, blessings, and invocations with the use of the document *Of Exorcisms and Certain Supplications*. In the modern era, Catholic bishops rarely authorize exorcisms, approaching would-be cases with the presumption that mental or physical illness is more likely.

Solemn exorcisms, according to the Canon law of the church, can be exercised only by an ordained priest (or higher prelate), with the express permission of the local bishop, and only after a careful medical examination to exclude the possibility of mental illness,[43] and in the ritual people cannot in any circumstance be harmed. The *Catholic Encyclopedia* (1908) enjoined: "Superstition ought not to be confounded with religion, however much their history may be interwoven, nor magic, however white it may be, with a legitimate religious rite." Things listed in the Roman Ritual as being indicators of possible demonic possession include: speaking foreign or ancient languages of which the possessed has no prior knowledge; supernatural abilities and strength; knowledge of hidden or remote things which the possessed has no way of knowing; an aversion to anything holy; and profuse blasphemy and/or sacrilege.

Fr. Gabriele Amorth, who claimed to have performed 160,000 exorcisms, said exorcists have the ability to detect an evil presence. However, he notes that "they are not always right: their 'feelings' must be checked out." In his examples, they are able to detect the events that caused the demon to enter, or are able to discover the evil object that has cursed the individual. He notes that "they are always humble."[44]

Eastern Orthodoxy

"
   Receive the exorcisms with devotion...Divine exorcisms, borrowed from the Scripture, purify the soul.
"

— St. Cyril of Jerusalem

In the Eastern Orthodox Church, demonic activity is inextricably associated with disease and blight. As a result, exorcisms are quite common, even finding their way in rituals involving the blessing of fields. The exorcism ritual, found in the *Euchologion*, is that of St. Basil the Great. The baptism liturgy in Eastern Orthodoxy also contains an exorcism ritual.

Lutheranism

The Lutheran Church traces the practice of exorcism to the Scriptural claim that Jesus Christ expelled demons with a simple command (Mark 1:23–26; 9:14–29; Luke 11:14–26). The apostles continued the practice with the power and in the name of Jesus (Matthew 10:1; Acts 19:11–16). Contrary to some denominations of Christianity, Lutheranism affirms that the individual, both the believer and the non-believer, can be plagued by demons, based on several arguments, including the one that "just as a believer, whom Jesus Christ has delivered from sin (Romans 6:18), can still be bound by sin in his life, so he can still be bound by a demon in his life."

After the Protestant Reformation, Martin Luther abbreviated the Roman ritual used for exorcism. In 1526, the ritual was further abbreviated and the exsufflation was omitted. This form of the *Lutheran Ritual for Exorcism* was incorporated into the majority of the Lutheran service-books and implemented. According to a Pastoral Handbook of the Lutheran Church, <templatestyles src="Template:Quote/styles.css"/>

> *In general, satanic possession is nothing other than an action of the devil by which, from God's permission, men are urged to sin, and he occupies their bodies, in order that they might lose eternal salvation. Thus bodily possession is an action by which the devil, from divine permission, possesses both pious and impious men in such a way that he inhabits their bodies not only according to activity, but also according to essence, and torments them, either for the punishment or for the discipline and testing of men, and for the glory of divine justice, mercy, power, and wisdom.*

These pastoral manuals warn that often, symptoms such as ecstasy, epileptic seizures, lethargy, insanity, and a frantic state of mind, are the results of natural causes and should not be mistaken for demon possession. According to the Lutheran Church, primary symptoms that may indicate demon possession and the need of an exorcism include:

1. The knowledge of secret things, for example, being able to predict the future (Acts 16:16), find lost people or things, or know complex things that one has never learned (e.g., medicine). It is said that fortune-tellers often ask a spirit for help and that this spirit gives them certain powers. In that case, the evil spirit is assisting, not necessarily possessing the person bodily.
2. The knowledge of languages one has never learned. Just as the devil can bind one's tongue (Luke 11:14), it is reported from the early church as well as the time of the Reformation that certain demon-possessed people could speak languages they had never learned.
3. Supernatural strength (Mark 5:2-3), far beyond what they previously had or should have considering their sex and size. Much caution in judging demon possession is required. All of the circumstances and symptoms must be taken into consideration. Insanity should not be confused with possession. On the other hand, possession may be taking place even where these symptoms are absent.

The Church lists the secondary symptoms of horrible shouting (Mark 5:5), blasphemy of God and jeering at one's neighbor, deformation of movements (e.g. ferocious movements, facial contortion, immodest laughing, gnashing of teeth, spitting, removing clothes, lacerating self, Mk. 9:20; Lk. 8:27.), inhuman revelry (e.g. when they take food beyond the capability of nature), torment of bodies, unusual injuries of the body and of those nearby, extraordinary motion of bodies (e.g., an elderly man who, being demon-possessed, was able to run as fast as a horse), and forgetfulness of things done. Other symptoms include the corruption of reason in man, which make him like an animal, melancholy, the acceleration of death (Mark 9:18 [suicide attempts]), and the presence of other supernatural occurrences.

After these determinations have been made, the Church recommends experienced physicians to determine whether there is a medical explanation for the behaviour of the individual. When a true possession is recognized, the poor one is to be committed to the care of a minister of the Church who teaches sound doctrine, is of a blameless life, who does nothing for the sake of filthy lucre, but does everything from the soul. The pastor is then to diligently inquire what kind of life the possessed one led up to this point and lead him or her through the law to the recognition of his sins. After this admonition or consolation has taken place, the works of a natural physician are to be used, who will cleanse the possessed one from malicious fluids with the appropriate medicines. The Pastoral Handbook then states: <templatestyles src="Template:Quote/styles.css"/>

- *Let ardent prayers be poured forth to God, not only by the ministers of the Church, but also by the whole Church. Let these prayers be conditioned, if the liberation should happen for God's glory and the salvation of the possessed person, for this is an evil of the body.*
- *With the prayers let fasting be joined, see Matthew 17:21.*
- *Alms by friends of the possessed person, Tobit 12:8-9.*
- *Let the confession of the Christian faith be once required of Him, let him be taught concerning the works of the devil destroyed by Christ, let him be sent back faithfully to this Destroyer of Satan, Jesus Christ, let an exhortation be set up to faith in Christ, to prayers, to penitence.*

Mennonites

Many Mennonite colleges and seminaries include training for the ministry of exorcism. The Mennonite minister and exorcist Dean Hochstetler states that powwowing, a practice done by some in the Pennsylvania Dutch community, "brings people under bondage to Satan." On 30 July to 1 August 1987, the "Associated Mennonite Biblical Seminaries, Mennonite Board of Missions (MC) and the Indiana-Michigan Mennonite Conference (MC) sponsored a consultation on 'Bondage and Deliverance'."

Methodism

The British Methodist Church holds that the ritual of exorcism involves "the casting out of an objective power of evil which has gained possession of a person." Moreover, the Methodist Church teaches that "the authority to exorcise has been given to the Church as one of the ways in which Christ's Ministry is continued in the world." A minister must first consult the District Chair in order to perform an exorcism. The Methodist Church holds that it is of great importance to ensure that the presence and love of Christ is assured to the individual(s) seeking help. In addition, the ministry of the "Bible, prayer and sacraments" should be extended to these individuals as well. A combination of these things has been proven to be effective.

For example, in one particular situation, a Roman Catholic woman believed that her house was haunted, and therefore consulted her priest for assistance. Since he was not available to drive the demons from the woman's home, she contacted a Methodist pastor, who exorcised the evil spirits from a room, which was believed to be the source of distress in the house, and celebrated Holy Communion in the same place; following these actions, there was no longer any problem in the house. In another situation, The Reverend Jay Bartlett writes that a young lady who was involved with "drug abuse, self mutilation, severe abuse, mental torment, Satanism, occult activity, communion with demons, and other evils" was exorcised at Mt. Olive Free Methodist Church in Dallas over a period of seven nights, with "anointing oil, the Word of God (the sword of the Spirit), holy water, the sacred symbols of the cross, the blood of Christ, and consecrated materials [being] utilized to drive out the demons."

Oriental Orthodoxy

In the Ethiopian Orthodox Tewahedo Church, priests intervene and perform exorcisms on behalf of those believed to be afflicted by demons or *buda*. According to a 2010 Pew Research Center study, 74% of Christians in Ethiopia claim to have experienced or witnessed an exorcism. Demon-possessed persons are brought to a church or prayer meeting.[45] Often, when an ill person has not responded to modern medical treatment, the affliction is attributed to demons. Unusual or especially perverse deeds, particularly when performed in public, are symptomatic of a demoniac. Superhuman strength – such as breaking one's bindings, as described in the New Testament accounts – along with glossolalia are observed in the afflicted. Amsalu Geleta, in a modern case study, relates elements that are common to Ethiopian Christian exorcisms:

> It includes singing praise and victory songs, reading from the Scripture, prayer and confronting the spirit in the name of Jesus. Dialogue with the spirit is another important part of the exorcism ceremony. It helps the

counselor (exorcist) to know how the spirit was operating in the life of the demoniac. The signs and events mentioned by the spirit are affirmed by the victim after deliverance.

The exorcism is not always successful, and Geleta notes another instance in which the usual methods were unsuccessful, and the demons apparently left the subject at a later time. In any event, "in all cases the spirit is commanded in no other name than the name of Jesus."

Pentecostalism

In the Pentecostal Church, Charismatic Movement, and other the less formalized sections of Christianity, the exorcism ritual can take many forms and belief structures. The most common of these is the deliverance ceremony. Deliverance differs from the exorcism ceremony in that the Devil may have gotten a foothold into a person's life rather than gaining complete control . If complete control has been gained, a full-fledged exorcism is necessary. However, a "spirit-filled Christian" cannot be possessed, based on their beliefs. Within this belief structure, the reasons for the devil to get a foothold are usually explained to be some sort of deviation from theological doctrine or because of pre-conversion activities (like dealing with the occult).[46,47]

The traditional method for determining if a person needs a deliverance is done by having someone present who has the gift of discerning of spirits. This is a gift of the Holy Spirit from 1 Corinthians 12 that allows a person to "sense" in some way an evil presence.[48] While the initial diagnosis is usually uncontested by the congregation, when many people are endowed with this gift in a single congregation, results may vary.[49]

Criticism

Critics of exorcism contend that so-called 'possession' is often, in fact, undiagnosed mental illness and the performance of an exorcism in such cases exacerbates the condition and can even be considered abuse.[50] There have also been cases where exorcists have abused their position for financial gain.[51]

Gallery

Figure 7: *A boy possessed by a demon*

Figure 8: *The Canaanite woman's daughter*

Figure 9: *The Gerasenes demonic*

Figure 10: *At the Synagogue in Capernaum*

Figure 11: *Christ exorcising at sunset*

Figure 12: *The blind and mute man*

Figure 13: *Exorcising a mute*

Figure 14: *Saint Francis exorcised demons in Arezzo, in a depiction on a fresco by Giotto.*

Further reading

- Lawrence Edward Burkholder (1999), *Let My People Go: A Mennonite Theology of Exorcism*[52] (PDF), Conrad Grebel College.
- Jay Bartlett (12 February 2010), *Exorcisms in the Methodist Church*, ISBN 9780557316236.

External links

- ⓘ Herbermann, Charles, ed. (1913). "Exorcism". *Catholic Encyclopedia*. New York: Robert Appleton Company.
- Diocese of Worcester webpages on Ministry of Deliverance[53] Anglican View
- Exorcism in the Orthodox Church[54]

Minor exorcism in Christianity

The expression **minor exorcism** can be used in a technical sense or a general sense. The general sense indicates any exorcism which is not a solemn exorcism of a person believed to be possessed, including various forms of deliverance ministry. This article deals only with the technical sense which specifically refers to certain prayers used with persons preparing to become baptised members of the Christian Church. These prayers request God's assistance so that the person to be baptised will be kept safe from the power of Satan or protected in a more general way from temptation.

Ancient practice

As early as the 3rd century of Western Christianity, there is evidence[55,56] of the existence of four minor orders of clergy in the Latin Church, one of which was entitled 'exorcist'. Pope Cornelius (251–253) noted that among the clergy in Rome there were fifty-two such exorcists, among other ministries listed,[57] and the institution of these orders, and the organization of their functions, seems to have been the work of Cornelius's predecessor, Pope Fabian (236–250).[58]

Text previously attributed to a fourth Council of Carthage in 398, now identified as a collection called *Statuta Ecclesiæ Antiqua*, prescribes in its seventh canon the rite of ordination of such an exorcist: the bishop is to give him the book containing the formulae of exorcism, saying, "Receive, and commit to memory, and possess the power of imposing hands on energumens, whether baptized or catechumens"; and the same rite was still in use in the early 20th

Figure 15: *In many Christian denominations, the minor exorcism in an integral part of the baptismal liturgy.*

century, except that instead of the ancient Book of Exorcisms, the Roman Pontifical, or Roman Missal, was placed into the hands of the ordinand. The same canons required that those preparing to be baptised (known as catechumens) were to undergo a daily imposition of hands by these exorcists.

The 4th century Mystagogical Catechesis of Cyril of Jerusalem gives a detailed description of baptismal exorcism, from which it appears that anointing with exorcised oil formed a part of this exorcism in the East.[59] Anointing with oil as part of baptismal exorcism is also mentioned in the Apostolic Tradition and the Arabic Canons of Hippolytus – early 20th Century scholarship attributed both of these documents to Hippolytus of Rome, but the origin of both sources is now disputed.

Authors such as Eusebius (3rd century) and Augustine (4th century) provide further details of these minor exorcisms, prayers and ceremonies performed over adults preparing for baptism. Eusebius mentions the imposition of hands and prayer. Among the Latins, and especially at Rome, breathing accompanied with a form of exorcism and placing in the mouth a little exorcised salt, was employed in addition to the signing with the cross and the imposition of hands. Mostly those in the minor order of exorcist performed the ceremony of exorcism, then a priest signed the catechumens with the cross and laid hands upon them. The final ceremony took place on Holy Saturday, when the priest himself performed the ceremony of exorcism.[60]

An *exsufflatio*, or out-breathing of the demon by the candidate, which was sometimes part of the ceremony, symbolized the renunciation of the Devil, while the *insufflatio*, or in-breathing of the Holy Spirit, by ministers and assistants, symbolised the infusion of sanctifying grace by the sacrament.[61] Augustine noted that rites of exorcism by exsufflation were also performed for the baptism of infants.[62]

After the English Reformation, the Anglican baptismal rite in the 1549 *Book of Common Prayer*, which was based on the Sarum Rite, "took place at the church door and included singing with the cross on forehead and breast and an exorcism." Similarly, the Lutheran Church, in its 1526 *Baptismal Booklet* contained a minor exorcism before the sign of the cross.

Most of these ancient ceremonies were retained in the rites still practiced by the Catholic Church in the first half of the 20th century.

Contemporary practice

Anglicanism

Today, in some provinces of the Anglican Communion, the "Anglican liturgy does not involve an explicit exorcism or rejection of evil, but does including a signing with the cross and the wish that baptism delivers one from "the powers of darkness." Others, such as the Anglican Church of Tanzania, however, provide for anointing and consignation that accompanies "the exorcism that follows the examination of the candidates".

Catholicism

In 1972, the minor orders were reformed; men preparing to be ordained as Catholic priests or deacons would no longer receive the minor order of exorcist; the minor orders of lector and acolyte were retained, but redesignated as *ministries*. It was left open to the Catholic bishops of individual countries to petition the Vatican to establish a *ministry of exorcist* if it seemed useful in that nation.[63] Since then, Pope Benedict XVI mandated that each diocese in the world should have at least one active exorcist, and encouraged training of priests by the International Association of Exorcists in Rome.

As part of the wider reforms of the Second Vatican Council, all Catholic liturgical books were updated, including the rites for the baptism of adults and of children. The revised rites retained prayers designated *minor exorcisms*, for use during or before the ceremony of baptism itself. These would be performed as a routine part of the normal preparation for Christian baptism.

In 1969, an English translation was released of the Rite of Baptism for Children (later amended 1984). Baptism could now be celebrated by a priest or deacon and included a formula of minor exorcism. This was located in the rite immediately following prayers for the child and a Litany of the Saints, and was immediately followed by an anointing with the oil of catechumens.

The Second Vatican Council also called[64] for adults seeking baptism to be part of a formal process of preparation, or catechumenate, as was the case in the early church. A Rite of Christian Initiation of Adults was therefore prepared after the Council, and an interim English edition published in 1974. A revised and expanded version for the USA was published in 1988. The rite includes a selection of eleven texts for minor exorcisms, which may be performed on one or more occasions during the months when a person enrolled as a catechumen is preparing for baptism.[65] Anointing with the oil of catechumens may be repeated on several occasions.[66] The notes also indicate that the minor exorcisms may be carried out by a lay catechist deputed for this purpose by the bishop, though the use of the oil of catechumens is reserved to deacons and priests.

In addition to these exorcisms, the Rite for Adults includes three ceremonies called scrutinies, to be celebrated as integral parts of the Sunday Eucharist on the Third, Fourth, and Fifth Sundays of Lent. Each scrutiny contain a prayer of exorcism reserved to the deacon or priest. There is also a simplified set of prayers provided for use with children mature enough to be personally catechised. The only minor exorcism in the children's rite is part of a one-off scrutiny which is offered in two forms. Both texts use the image of entering the light of Christ, turning respectively from "darkness" and from "whatever could make them bad".[67]

The USA ritual book also contains additional prayers to be used with already-baptised Christians preparing to be received into full communion with the Catholic Church, including a one-off scrutiny which may be celebrated on the Second Sunday of Lent. Although it notes that a careful distinction must be made between the exorcisms of catechumens and this penitential rite for baptised adults, one possible prayer over the candidates prays that the candidates may "be freed of ... obstacles and falsehoods" while the other prays that they may "resist all that is deceitful and harmful" and that Jesus would "heal the wounds of their sins".[68]

Lutheranism

In the Lutheran Church, through its Rite of Exorcism in the Baptismal Liturgy, "the Church has kept an opportunity to teach how serious this falleness' is, and can, through bold proclamations against the devil, teach what a blessing and joy it is to receive the Holy Spirit with the Water and Word of Holy Baptism. Rather than inviting the devil into one by ignoring his presence in all the unbaptized, the Church proclaims boldly his overthrow (James 4:7), and reminds herself, and all her members, who our enemies truly are: the devil, the world, and, yes, even our own sinful flesh. And, the Good News that one dies with Christ, and rises to new life in Him with the Water and the Word, brings us comfort in our battles with our defeated enemies (Romans 6:4; 16:20)."

Methodism

The baptismal liturgy, used in the United Methodist Church, contains a minor exorcism, when the candidate for baptism is asked to reject the 'spiritual forces of wickedness and evil powers of this world'.

References

This article incorporates text from a publication now in the public domain: Herbermann, Charles, ed. (1913). "article name needed". *Catholic Encyclopedia*. New York: Robert Appleton.

Exorcism in the Catholic Church

The Catholic Church authorizes the use of exorcism for those who are believed to be the victims of demonic possession. In Roman Catholicism, exorcism is sacramental[69,70] but not a sacrament, unlike baptism or confession. Unlike a sacrament, exorcism's "integrity and efficacy do not depend ... on the rigid use of an unchanging formula or on the ordered sequence of prescribed actions. Its efficacy depends on two elements: authorization from valid and licit Church authorities, and the faith of the exorcist."[71] The Catechism of the Catholic Church states: "When the Church asks publicly and authoritatively in the name of Jesus Christ that a person or object be protected against the power of the Evil One and withdrawn from his dominion, it is called exorcism."

The Catholic Church revised the Rite of Exorcism in January 1999, though the traditional Rite of Exorcism in Latin is allowed as an option. The ritual assumes that possessed persons retain their free will, though the demon may hold control over their physical body, and involves prayers, blessings, and invocations with the use of the document *Of Exorcisms and Certain Supplications*.

Figure 16: *Painting by Francisco Goya of Saint Francis Borgia performing an exorcism.*

Solemn exorcisms, according to the Canon law of the Church, can be exercised only by an ordained priest (or higher prelate), with the express permission of the local bishop, and only after a careful medical examination to exclude the possibility of mental illness.[72] The *Catholic Encyclopedia* (1908) enjoined: "Superstition ought not to be confounded with religion, however much their history may be interwoven, nor magic, however white it may be, with a legitimate religious rite." Things listed in the Roman Ritual as being indicators of possible demonic possession include: speaking foreign or ancient languages of which the possessed has no prior knowledge; supernatural abilities and strength; knowledge of hidden or remote things which the possessed has no way of knowing; an aversion to anything holy; and profuse blasphemy and/or sacrilege.

History

The first official guidelines for exorcism were established in 1614. They were later revised by the Vatican in 1999 as the demand for exorcisms increased. In the 15th century, Catholic exorcists were both priestly and lay, since every Christian was considered as having the power to command demons and drive them out in the name of Christ. These exorcists used the Benedictine formula

"*Vade retro satana*" ("Step back, Satan") around this time. By the late 1960s, Roman Catholic exorcisms were seldom performed in the United States, but by the mid-1970s, popular film and literature revived interest in the ritual, with thousands claiming demonic possession. Maverick priests who belonged to fringes took advantage of the increase in demand and performed exorcisms with little or no official sanction. The exorcisms that they performed were, according to *Contemporary American Religion*, "clandestine, underground affairs, undertaken without the approval of the Catholic Church and without the rigorous psychological screening that the church required. In subsequent years, the Church took more aggressive action on the demon-expulsion front. The practice of exorcism without consent from the Catholic Church is what prompted the official guidelines from 1614 to be amended. The amendment established the procedure that clergy members and each individual who claims to be impacted by demonic possession must follow. This includes the rule that the potentially possessed individual must be evaluated by a medical professional before any other acts are taken. The primary reason for this action is to eliminate any suspicion of mental illness, before the next steps of the procedure are taken. Since demonic possession is extremely rare, and mental health issues are often mistaken for demonic possession, the Vatican requires that each diocese have a specially trained priest who is able to diagnose demonic possession and perform exorcisms when necessary. "

When an exorcism is needed

According to the Vatican guidelines issued in 1999, "the person who claims to be possessed must be evaluated by doctors to rule out a mental or physical illness." Most reported cases do not require an exorcism because twentieth-century Catholic officials regard genuine demonic possession as an extremely rare phenomenon that is easily confounded with natural mental disturbances. Despite that fact, every diocese is required to have at least one priest that is an exorcist, or is trained to perform exorcisms (17). As the demand for exorcisms has increased over the past few decades, the number of trained exorcists has also risen. In prior times, exorcists were kept fairly anonymous, and the performance of exorcisms remained a secret. Some exorcists attribute the rise in demand of exorcisms to the rise in drug abuse and violence, which leads to the suggestion that such things might work hand in hand. Many times a person just needs spiritual or medical help, especially if drugs or other addictions are present. The specially trained priest and medical professionals will be able to work together to address the patient, and be able to determine what type of illness the patient is suffering from. After the need of the person has been determined then the appropriate help will be met. In the circumstance of spiritual help, prayers may be offered, or the laying on of hands or a counseling

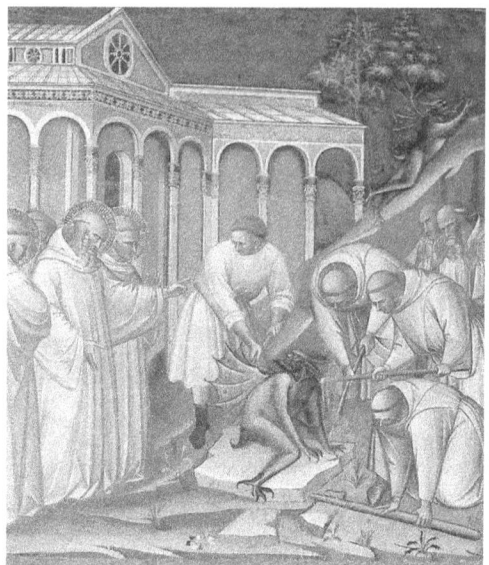

Figure 17: *Exorcism of St Benedict by Spinello Aretino, 1387.*

session may be prescribed. The exorcist might not perform an exorcism if he does not know the person.

Signs

Signs of demonic invasion vary depending on the type of demon and its purpose, including:

1. Loss or lack of appetite
2. Cutting, scratching, and biting of skin
3. A cold feeling in the room
4. Unnatural bodily postures and change in the person's face and body
5. The possessed losing control of their normal personality and entering into a frenzy or rage, and/or attacking others
6. Change in the person's voice
7. Supernatural physical strength not subject to the person's build or age
8. Speaking or understanding another language which they had never learned before
9. Knowledge of things that are distant or hidden
10. Prediction of future events (sometimes through dreams)
11. Levitation and moving of objects / things
12. Expelling of objects / things

Figure 18: *Saint Philip of Agira with the Gospel in his left hand, the symbol of the exorcists, in the May celebrations in his honor at Limina, Sicily*

13. Intense hatred and violent reaction toward all religious objects or items
14. Antipathy towards entering a church, speaking Jesus' name or hearing scripture.

Process of the exorcism

In the process of an exorcism the person possessed may be restrained so that they do not harm themselves or any person present. The exorcist then prays and commands for the demons to retreat. The Catholic Priest recites certain prayers the Our Father, Hail Mary, and the Athanasian Creed. Exorcists follow procedures listed in the ritual of the exorcism revised by the Vatican in 1999. Seasoned exorcists use the Rituale Romanum as a starting point, not always following the prescribed formula exactly.[73] *The Gale Encyclopedia of the Unusual and Unexplained* describes that an exorcism was a confrontation and not simply a prayer and once it has begun it has to finish no matter how long it takes. If the exorcist stops the rite, then the demon will pursue him which is why the process being finished is so essential. After the exorcism has been finished the person possessed feels a "kind of release of guilt and feels reborn and freed of sin." Not all exorcisms are successful the first time; it could take days, weeks, or months of constant prayer and exorcisms.

Literature

On this subject, there is the book by journalist Matt Baglio[74] called *The Rite: The Making of a Modern Exorcist*, first edited in 2009 and then in 2010, which inspired the film *The Rite*.[75,76,77,78]

Notable examples

- 1928 — Emma Schmidt underwent a 14-day exorcism performed by Catholic priest Theophilus Riesinger.
- 1949 — Roland Doe was allegedly possessed and underwent exorcism. The events later inspired the novel and film *The Exorcist*.
- 1975-1976 — Anneliese Michel was a woman from Germany who underwent 67 exorcisms, which inspired the films *The Exorcism of Emily Rose* and *Requiem*. In a conference several years later, German bishops retracted the claim that she was possessed.

Saint Padre Pio, a monk and mystic, was said to have exorcised a demon by saying "long live Jesus, long live Maria (Mary)"[Citation needed]

Further reading

- Baglio, Matt (2009). *The Rite: The Making of a Modern Exorcist*. Doubleday.
- Blatty, William Peter (1972). *The Exorcist*. Bantam Books.
- Dickason, C. Fred (1989). *Demon Possession & The Christian*. Crossway Books.
- Karpel, Craig (1975). *The Rite of Exorcism: The Complete Text*. Berkley Books.
- Kinnaman, Gary (1994). *Angels Dark and Light*. Servant Publications.
- McGinn, Bernard (1994). *Antichrist: Two Thousand Years of the Human Fascination with Evil*. HarperSanFrancisco.
- MacNutt, Francis (1995). *Deliverance from Evil*.
- Martin, Malachi (1976). *Hostage to the Devil: The Possession and Exorcism of Five Living Americans*.
- Nicola, John J. (1974). *Diabolical Possession and Exorcism*.
- Richardson, James T.; Best, Joel; Bromley, David G., eds. (1991). *The Satanism Scare*.

External links

- Frequently Asked Questions About Exorcism[79]—U.S. Conference of Catholic Bishops
- ⓘ Herbermann, Charles, ed. (1913). "Exorcism". *Catholic Encyclopedia*. New York: Robert Appleton Company.
- The Catholic Prayer of Exorcism in Latin .Prof Wladimir Di Giorgio.[80]
- What is an exorcism?[81]

In Islam

Exorcism in Islam

Exorcism in Islam is called *ruqya shar'iyah* (Arabic: رقية شرعية IPA: [ruqya sharʕiya]), and is thought to repair damage believed caused by jinn posession witchcraft (*shir*) or the evil eye.wikipedia:Citation needed Exorcisms today are part of a wider body of contemporary Islamic alternative medicine called *al-Tibb al-Nabawi* (Medicine of the Prophet).

Islamic religious context

Belief in Jinns, and other supernatural beings, is widespread in the Islamic world. Jinn is an Arabic collective noun deriving from the Semitic root jnn (Arabic: جَنّ / جِنّ, *jann*), whose primary meaning is "to hide".:68:193:341 Some authors interpret the word to mean, literally, "beings that are concealed from the senses". Such creatures are believed to inhabit desolate, dingy, dark places where they are feared. Jinn exist invisibly amongst humans, only detectable with the sixth sense. The jinn are subtile creatures created from *smokeless fire* (fire and air) thought to be able to possess animate and inanimate objects. Unlike demons, they are not necessarily evil, but own a capacity of free-will.[82]

Reasons for possession

Possession is not caused by Satan,[83] who is said to be just a tempter, whispering evil suggestions into humans heart, but, even though not mentioned in canonical scriptures, according to folklore by jinn, who can enter a human body physically or haunting them mentally. A possession by a jinn can happen for various reasons. Ibn Taymiyyah explained a Jinn could sometimes haunt an individual, because the person could (even unintentionally) harm the jinn; urinating or throwing hot water on it, or even killing a related jinn without even realizing it.[84]WP:NOTRS In this case the jinn will try to take revenge on the

Figure 19: *The 72nd chapter of the Qur'an entitled Al-Jinn (The Jinn), as well as the heading and introductory bismillah of the next chapter entitled al-Muzzammil (The Enshrouded One).*

person. Another cause for jinn possession is when a jinn falls in love with a human and thereupon the jinn possesses the human.[85] WP:NOTRS Some women have told of their experiences with jinn possession; where the jinn tried to have sexual interaction from inside their bodies.[86] WP:NOTRS Thirdly, it occurs when a jinn is evil and simply wants to harm a human for no specific reason, it will possess that person, if it gets the opportunity, while the human is in a very emotional state or unconsciousness.WP:NOTRS Jinn may also haunt someone in service of a sorcerer.

Signs of possession

In Islamic belief, there are different signs of possession for example:WP:NOTRS

- Procrastination in doing good acts or praying
- Constant laziness
- Recurring aggression
- Loss of senses while awake
- Constant headaches
- Recurring nightmares

- Laughing while asleep
- Sleepwalking

In case of a "complete control" by the Jinn, the possessed surrender to the Jinn and the persons consciousness is subverted by it. Such a jinn is indeed absolutely evil and thereupon the acts of the person are going to be evil as well. The person will obey the commands of the jinn at anytime. In a "constant possession" the person will not act without a command by the jinn.Wikipedia:Citation needed

According to reports of individuals who have claimed to be possessed, they've asserted that during the jinn possession their spiritual abilities, like the sixth sense, had increased. Possession can also cause physical damage, such as inexplicable bruising or marks appearing spontaneously.[87]

Procedure

Recited formulas, referred to as *Ruqyah* are used to expel the Jinn from the body. Majority of Ruqyah are either charms or spells that are uttered or written. *Nushrah* refers to charms or amulets that are used.Wikipedia:Citation needed

In a typical Islamic exorcism the treated person lies down while a white-gloved therapist places a hand on their head while reciting verses from the Quran.

Specific verses from the Quran are recited, which glorify God (e.g. The Throne Verse (Arabic: آية الكرسي *Ayatul Kursi*) and invoke his help. In some cases the *adhan* (call for daily prayers) is also read, believed to have the effect of repelling non-angelic unseen beings or the *jinn*.Wikipedia:Citation needed

The Islamic prophet Muhammad taught his followers to read the last three *suras* from the Quran, Surat al-Ikhlas (The Fidelity), Surat al-Falaq (The Dawn) and Surat an-Nas (Mankind).Wikipedia:Citation needed

A common healing practice in classical Islam used music to cure mental illnesses, related to jinn-possession.[88]Wikipedia:Verifiability

Islamic Exorcists

Those who are permitted to perform exorcisms typically have other careers but possess the ability to exorcise.Wikipedia:Verifiability

Exorcism and Islamic Law

Prohibited techniques often utilize *shirk*, which is found in practices that prepare amulets or talismans. This is prohibited because *shirk* is the sin of practicing idolatry or polytheism i.e. the deification or worship of anyone or anything besides the singular God. Many times Qur'anic verses are added throughout the recitation when using these objects in order to 'mask' their *shirk*. However, God believes he has provided sufficient cures in executing an exorcism, therefore exorcists should not have to rely on methods involving *shirk*. Additionally, individuals seeking exorcism should avoid magicians or soothsayers because these magical practices go against Islamic Law.Wikipedia:Citation needed

Hadith of the 70,000 who do not ask for *ruqya* and will not be brought to account

A *hadith* recorded in *Sahih al-Bukhari*, 8:76:479[89] states: "Seventy thousand people of my followers will enter Paradise without accounts, and they are those who do not practice Ar-Ruqya and do not see an evil omen in things, and put their trust in their Lord." Ibn Qayyim al-Jawziyya, a scholar, commented on this *hadith*, stating: "That is because these people will enter Paradise without being called to account because of the perfection of their Tawheed, therefore he described them as people who did not ask others to perform ruqyah for them. Hence he said "and they put their trust in their Lord." Because of their complete trust in their Lord, their contentment with Him, their faith in Him, their being pleased with Him and their seeking their needs from Him, they do not ask people for anything, be it ruqyah or anything else, and they are not influenced by omens and superstitions that could prevent them from doing what they want to do, because superstition detracts from and weakens Tawheed".

Popularity of Islamic alternative medicine

The trend in *al-Tibb al-Nabawi* treatments, cosmetics and toiletries is often associated with fundamentalists who charge that Western, chemically laced prescriptions aim to poison Muslims or defile them with insulin and other medicines made from pigs. Members of terrorist groups have been involved in Islamic remedies as healers and sellers, while some clinics are used as recruiting grounds for Islamist causes.

"Islamic medicine carries a cachet that, by taking it, you are reinforcing your faith – and the profits go to Muslims," says Sidney Jones, an expert on Islam in Southeast Asia with the International Crisis Group.

Exorcism in Islam 43

Figure 20: *Ali and the Jinn, Golestan Palace, Iran, 1568.*

External links

- *Ruqyah* treatment[90]
- Ruqya treatment for *evil eye*[91]
- How to become a Raqi[92]

In Buddhism

Ghosts in Tibetan culture

There is widespread belief in **ghosts in Tibetan culture**. Ghosts are explicitly recognized in the Tibetan Buddhist religion as they were in Indian Buddhism, occupying a distinct but overlapping world to the human one, and feature in many traditional legends. When a human dies, after a period of uncertainty they may enter the ghost world. A hungry ghost (Tibetan: *yidag, yi-dvags*; Sanskrit: *preta*, प्रेत) has a tiny throat and huge stomach, and so can never be satisfied. Ghosts may be killed with a ritual dagger or caught in a spirit trap and burnt, thus releasing them to be reborn. Ghosts may also be exorcised, and an annual festival is held throughout Tibet for this purpose. Some say that Dorje Shugden, the ghost of a powerful 17th-century monk, is a deity, but the Dalai Lama asserts that he is a wrathful spirit, which has caused a split in the Tibetan exile community.

Nature of ghosts

Tibetan Buddhists believe that when a person dies, they enter the intermediate *Bardo* state, from which they may be reborn in this world in a human or animal body, in the ghost world in a ghost body, in one of the paradise realms or in one of the hells. But eventually, the person will die in this after-death world and be reborn as a human or other creature unless they achieve *Nirvana*, where they are beyond all states of embodiment.

Hungry ghosts have their own realm depicted on the Bhavacakra and are represented as teardrop or paisley-shaped with bloated stomachs and necks too thin to pass food, so that attempting to eat is also incredibly painful. Some are described as having "mouths the size of a needle's eye and a stomach the size of a mountain". This is a metaphor for people futilely attempting to fulfill their illusory physical desires. Sometime individuals have a predominance of hungry ghost in their makeup. They can never get enough, and are always hungry

Figure 21: *Tibetan ghost Nam-khyi nag-po according to an old Tibetan blockprint of the Vaidurya dkar-po (1685)*

for more. The Tibetan word for the emotional state of the hungry ghost, *ser na*, literally means "yellow nosed", and could be said to mean "meanness" or "lack of generosity". The person in this state is constantly seeking to consume and to enrich themselves, but can never be satisfied.

A tulpa is a type of ghost or being that is created through mental effort, purely from the thoughts of its creator. A very skilled Buddhist practitioner or sorcerer may have this ability, and in some cases a Tulpa may be created from the collective thoughts of the villagers. Such a ghost is not self-aware at first, but may gradually acquire awareness and go on to become a normal human being.

Dealing with ghosts

Phurba

The *phurba* (Tibetan: ཕུར་བ, Sanskrit: *kīla*) is a ritual dagger used by a tantric practitioner to release an evil spirit from its suffering and guide it to a better rebirth. Such a spirit (ghost) is a being which lingers in confusion between different realms. By plunging the dagger into it, it is thrown out of its confusion and gets the chance to be reborn, probably as a lower kind than human.

Spirit traps

Families often mount ghost-traps on the roofs of their houses, spindle-like contraptions wound with colored yarns. A spirit trap may also be hung in a tree. The series of interlocking threads is thought to ensnare the spirit, and is burnt when the job is done.

Exorcising-Ghost day

The Tibetan religious ceremony 'Gutor' ⟨དགུ་གཏོར་⟩, literally offering of the 29th, is held on the 29th of the 12th Tibetan month, with its focus on driving out all negativity, including evil spirits and misfortunes of the past year, and starting the new year in a peaceful and auspicious way.

The temples and monasteries throughout Tibet hold grand religious dance ceremonies, with the largest at Potala Palace in Lhasa. Families clean their houses on this day, decorate the rooms and eat a special noodle soup called 'Guthuk'. ⟨དགུ་ཐུག་⟩ In the evening, the people carry torches, calling out the words of exorcism.

A folk tale

A story tells of a man who met a ghost while out walking. The ghost started walking with him, which made him very frightened, although he hid his fear and pretended that he too was a ghost. They came to a town. The ghost left the man resting, entered the town and stole the soul of the king's son, tying it up in a yak hair sack. Returning to the man, the ghost left the sack in his care for a while. The man took the sack into the town, where the king was in great alarm because his son was dying. The man promised to revive the boy, conducting rituals and at the same time releasing the boy's soul from the bag. When the boy revived, the king gave the man half of all his property as reward.

Dorje Shugden

Dorje Shugden is the ghost of a powerful 17th-century monk who was murdered in his palace in Tibet. His adherents consider that he is a deity. However, in the late 1970s the Dalai Lama reconsidered his faith in Dorje Shugden, and decided that the wrathful spirit was working against him, hampering his goal of seeking autonomy for Tibet with minimal interference from Beijing. This has caused a split between Tibetan exiles, with often bitter arguments between those who follow the Dalai Lama and those who continue to revere Dorje Shugden. The Western Shugden Society is one of these organizations.

Figure 22: *Statue of Dorje Shugden*

Notable exorcisms and exorcists

Louviers possessions

The possessions at Louviers (Normandy, France), similar to those in Aix-en-Provence, occurred at the Louviers Convent in 1647. As with both the Aix case and its later counterpart in Loudun, the conviction of the priests involved hinged on the confessions of possessed demoniacs.

Accusations

Sister Madeleine Bavent was 18 years old in 1625; the initial possession victim, she claimed to have been bewitched by Mathurin Picard, the nunnery's director, and Father Thomas Boulle, the vicar of Louviers. Her confession to authorities claimed that the two men had abducted her and taken her to a witches' sabbat. There, she was married to the Devil, whom she called "Dagon", and committed sexual acts with him on the altar. Two men were allegedly crucified and disemboweled as these acts took place.

Madeleine's confession prompted the investigation, which found that other nuns were also victims of Picard and Boulle; they also reported having been brought to secret sabbats where sexual intercourse with demons, particularly Dagon, took place. These confessions were accompanied by what investigators believed were classic signs of demonic possession: contortions, unnatural body movements, speaking in tongues (glossolalia), obscene insults, blasphemies, and the appearance of unexplainable wounds that vanished without aid.

Beyond mere symptoms of possession, the body of Sister Barbara of St. Michael was said to be possessed by a specific demon named Ancitif.

Exorcisms

As in the Loudun possessions a decade prior, the exorcisms at Louviers were a public spectacle. Nearly every person present at the exorcisms was questioned by the inquisitors, and the entire town of Louviers began exhibiting symptoms of hysteria as the cries of the nuns undergoing exorcism rose with the screams of Father Boulle, who was tortured at the same time; Mathurin Picard had died previous to the public display.

Father Bosroger recorded the proceedings, which he would publish in 1652. In his account, nuns were said to confess further evidence against Picard and Boulle. In addition to tempting them into sexual acts, Satan (supposedly in the form of Picard and Boulle) had also tried leading the nuns down the road of heresy. Appearing to the nuns as a beautiful angel, the Devil engaged them in theological conversations so clever that they began to doubt their own teachings. When told that this was not the same information they had been taught, Satan replied that he was a messenger of heaven who was sent to reveal fatal errors in what was otherwise accepted dogma.

Signs of possession continued throughout the exorcisms. One witness wrote that a nun "ran with movements so abrupt that it was difficult to stop her. One of the clerics present, having caught her by the arm, was surprised to find that it did not prevent the rest of her body from turning over and over as if the arm were fixed to the shoulder merely by a spring."

Punishment

As hysteria rose, it seemed inevitable that a trial would occur and Father Boulle's fate would be sealed. During the exorcisms, though, parliament at Rouen passed sentence: Sister Madeleine Bavent would be imprisoned for life in the church dungeon, Father Thomas Boulle would be burnt alive, and the corpse of Mathurin Picard would be exhumed and burned.

Catalogue

After the nuns at Louviers were afflicted, authorities undertook the task of cataloguing the symptoms of demonic possession. The treatise they developed included fifteen indications of true possession:

1. To think oneself possessed.
2. To lead a wicked life.
3. To live outside the rules of society.

4. To be persistently ill, falling into heavy sleep and vomiting unusual objects (either such natural objects as toads, serpents, maggots, iron, stones, and so forth; or such artificial objects as nails, pins, etc.).
5. To utter obscenities and blasphemies.
6. To be troubled with spirits ("an absolute and inner possession and residence in the body of the person").
7. To show a frightening and horrible countenance.
8. To be tired of living.
9. To be uncontrollable and violent.
10. To make sounds and movements like an animal.
11. To deny knowledge of fits after the paroxysm has ended.
12. To show fear of sacred relics and sacraments.
13. To curse violently at any prayer.
14. To exhibit acts of lewd exposure or abnormal strength.

Modern viewpoints

It is widely believed today that the Louviers Possessions, similar in many ways to those at Aix-en-Provence (1611), Lille (1613), and Loudun (1634) were part of a political and religious "show" in France.

They also differ from later cases of possession and witch-hunt hysteria like that in England and Colonial America in that they involve lurid sex themes. During the exorcisms at Louviers, nuns were seen to raise their habits and beg for sexual attention, use vulgar language, and make lascivious movements. In the earlier case at Loudun, a local doctor named Claude Quillet wrote, "These poor little devils of nuns, seeing themselves shut up within four walls, become madly in love, fall into a melancholic delirium, worked upon by the desires of the flesh, and in truth, what they need to be perfectly cured is a remedy of the flesh."

Most demonic possessions in France of this period (from the early to late 17th century) were of young women and appeared most often in the convents. Physicians and psychologists today attribute much of the activities to sexual hysteria, alluded to so long ago by Quillet.

Extreme seizures explained in the 17th century are today believed to point to epilepsy and similar diseases. In the time-frame of the cases in France, demonic possession served as a catchall explanation for any personality anomaly.

References

- Summers, Montague (1927). *The Geography of Witchcraft*. History of Civilization. London: Routledge and Kegan Paul.
- Michelet, Jules (1939) [1862]. *La Sorcière [Satanism and Witchcraft]*. Translated by A.R. Allinson. Reprint, Secaucus, N.J.: Citadel Press, 1992

Aix-en-Provence possessions

The **Aix-en-Provence possessions** were a series of alleged cases of demonic possession occurring among the Ursuline nuns of Aix-en-Provence (South of France) in 1611. Father Louis Gaufridi was accused and convicted of causing the possession by a pact with the devil, and he was executed by being burned at the stake, atop a pile of bushes because they burned slower and hotter than logs. This case provided the legal precedent for the conviction and execution of Urbain Grandier at Loudun more than 20 years later. In both cases, sexual themes dominated the manifestations of the possessions.

Diabolical invasion

The first 20–25 years of the 17th century were host to the peak of accusations in France's witchcraft hunt. During this time-frame, the number of cases involving demonic possession, priests and nuns outnumber that of any other period.

Madeleine de Demandolx

Signs of a demon invasion were believed to appear at Aix-en-Provence during the year 1609 through the victim Madeleine de Demandolx de la Palud. Madeleine, a 17-year-old Ursuline nun with a history of emotional instability, was returned often to the care of her parents to recover from attacks of depression. Father Louis Gaufridi was a friend of Madeleine's family and it is believed that he and Madeleine became lovers.

This rumor reached the ears of Sister Catherine de Gaumer, head of the Ursuline convent at Marseilles. She passed the rumor on to Madeleine's mother, and words were conveyed to Father Gaufridi that his attentions should cease immediately.

It was then that Madeleine was admitted to the Ursuline convent at Marseilles, under the direct supervision of Mother de Gaumer. To de Gaumer, Madeleine revealed the full story of her relations with Father Gaufridi. In order to prevent further damage and to halt any association with Father Gaufridi, Madeleine was transferred to the distant convent at Aix. Two years later, at the age of 19, Madeleine fell victim to what those around her considered to be unmistakable demonic possession; her body was contorted, and in a fit of rage she destroyed a crucifix.

Common convent practice at the time prescribed an exorcism to banish Madeleine's demons. Not only were the first attempts futile, but further attempts brought damning accusations that Father Gaufridi was a devil worshipper that had copulated with her since she was 17. Three more nuns were soon found to be possessed by demons, and by the end of the year that number had risen to eight. Sister Louise Capeau was considered to be the most extremely afflicted; her ravings and bodily contortions were more hideous than Madeleine's.

Inquisition at Aix-en-Provence

With the situation at the Ursuline convent getting out of control, Father Romillon enlisted the aid of the Grand Inquisitor Sebastien Michaelis. A Flemish exorcist, Father Domptius, was called upon to continue attempts at removing the demons from the possessed nuns.

After Vérin, the demon in possession of Madeleine, accused Father Gaufridi of causing her possession,[93] reporting to the amazed exorcist Father Domptius that 666 demons were in possession of her body, Gaufridi was summoned from his parish to exorcise Sister Louise Capeau. For his efforts, the priest was rewarded with denouncement as a sorcerer and cannibal. To the dangerous accusation, Gaufridi replied, "If I were a witch, I would certainly give my soul to a thousand devils." Taken by the inquisitors as a confession of guilt, Gaufridi was immediately imprisoned.

During this time, the possessed Sister Louise Capeau insisted loudly that Gaufridi had committed every imaginable form of sexual perversion, alarming authorities into searching the priest's rooms for magical books or objects. They found nothing incriminating, and were told by his parish that he was a well regarded man.

After being released to his parish, Father Gaufridi demanded his name be cleared and that his accusers be punished. The Grand Inquisitor remained determined that he would bring Gaufridi to trial. In 1611 Gaufridi was brought before a court in Aix.

Trial at Aix-en-Provence

Court proceedings saw both Sisters Madeline and Louise behave in, according to 17th century standards, a fashion typical of an advanced state of possession. Madeleine in particular was seen to maniacally swing from violently denouncing Gaufridi as a devil worshipper and sorcerer to retracting the accusations. She would return to charges of cannibalism, and then turn to begging him for a single word of kindness. Twice, Madeleine attempted suicide after the courts found the Devil's Mark on her body.

Father Gaufridi entered the courtroom after a series of physical and mental torture inflicted during his time in prison. His body had been shaved in a search for the Devil's Mark, three of which were found and used as evidence against him. A pact with the Devil was produced in court, allegedly signed by Gaufridi's own blood. A confession was also produced, which Gaufridi had signed in prison, extracted under torture. Included in the confession was an admission of celebrating a Black Mass in order to gain power over women:

"More than a thousand persons have been poisoned by the irresistible attraction of my breath which filled them with passion. The Lady of la Palud, the mother of Madeleine, was fascinated like so many others. But Madeleine was taken with an unreasoned love and abandoned herself to me both in the Sabbath and outside the Sabbath...I was marked at the Sabbath of my contentment and I had Madeleine marked on her head, on her belly, on her legs, on her thighs, on her feet..."

In court, Father Gaufridi strongly recanted the confession extracted from him by torture. In the eyes of the court and 17th century Christians, the protest was useless: the signed confession and alleged pact were evidence weighty enough to sentence the priest to death by fire. Even after the sentence was given, inquisitors continued to demand the names of Gaufridi's accomplices.

The sentence of Aix-en-Provence

April 30, 1611, was the day of Father Gaufridi's execution. With head and feet bare, a rope around his neck, Gaufridi officially asked pardon of God and was handed over to torturers. Still living after the torture of strappado and squassation, Gaufridi was escorted by archers while dragged through the streets of Aix for five hours before arriving at the place of execution. The priest was granted the mercy of strangulation before his body was burned to ashes.

Sister Madeleine Demandolx de la Palud renounced God and the saints before the church, going so far as to renounce all prayers ever said on her behalf and immediately following Gaufridi's execution was suddenly free of all possession. Her fellow demoniac, Sister Louise Capeau, was possessed until she died. Both of the sisters were banished from the convent, but Madeleine remained under the watch of the Inquisition. She was charged with witchcraft in 1642 and again in 1652. During her second trial, Madeleine was again found to have the Devil's mark and was sentenced to imprisonment. At an advanced age, she was released to the custody of a relative and died in 1670 at the age of 77.

Aix-en-Provence sets precedent

The Aix case was the first in which the testimony of an allegedly possessed person was taken into account. Prior to the 17th century, a demonically possessed (demoniac) person was considered unreliable when they laid accusations because most clerics believed that any words spoken by the demoniac were from the mouth of "the father of lies" (John 8:44). By its very nature, the utterances of a demoniac was not considered able to stand up as evidence.

The hysteria begun at Aix did not end with Gaufridi's sentence and the banishment of the nuns. In 1613, two years later, the possession hysteria spread to Lille where three nuns reported that Sister Marie de Sains had bewitched them. Sister Marie's testimony was a near copy of Sister Madeleine's renouncement two years earlier.

More than 20 years later, in 1634, the Aix-en-Provence possessions set precedent for the conviction and execution of Urbain Grandier.

References

- Cavendish, Richard. Man, Myth & Magic: The Illustrated Encyclopedia of Mythology, Religion, and the Unknown[94]. Toronto, Canada: Marshall Cavendish Limited. 1985.
- Baroja, Julio Caro. The World of the Witches. 1961. Reprint, Chicago: University of Chicago Press, 1975.

Loudun possessions

The **Loudun possessions** was a notorious witchcraft trial in Loudun, France in 1634. A convent of Ursuline nuns said they had been visited and possessed by demons. Following an investigation by the Catholic Church, a local priest named Father Urbain Grandier was accused of summoning the evil spirits. He was eventually convicted of the crimes of sorcery and burned at the stake.

The case contains similar themes to other witchcraft trials that occurred throughout western Europe in the 17th century, such as the Aix-en-Provence possessions (France) in 1611 or the Pendle witches (England) in 1612 before reaching the New World by the 1690s.

Early trials and conspiracy

The pact was allegedly signed between Urbain Grandier and the Devil, stolen from the Devil's cabinet of pacts by the demon Asmodeus. This page shows the signatures of all demons in possession of the Ursuline nuns at Loudun and the note added *Dictionnaire infernal* by Collin de Plancy (1826)

Urbain Grandier was appointed parish priest of St-Pierre-du-Marché in Loudun, a town in Poitou, France, in 1617. Grandier was considered to be a very good-looking man, and was both wealthy and well-educated. The combination made the priest a target for the attention of girls in Loudun, one of whom was Philippa Trincant, the daughter of the King's solicitor in Loudun. It was believed by the people of Loudun that Grandier was the father of Trincant's child. In addition to Trincant, Grandier openly courted Madeleine de Brou, daughter of the King's councillor in Loudun. Most assumed that Madeleine was Grandier's mistress after he wrote a treatise against the celibacy of priests for her.

Grandier was also a very well-connected man, high in political circles. When he was arrested and found guilty of immorality on June 2, 1630, it was these connections that restored him to full clerical duties within the same year. Presiding over the case was Chasteigner de La Roche Posay, the Bishop of Poitiers, a man who was known to dislike Grandier and admitted to wanting him out of the parish.

Two stories exist about what happened next. Either the Bishop of Poitiers approached Father Jean Mignon, confessor to the Ursuline nuns, and a plan was made to persuade a few of the sisters to feign possession and denounce Grandier, or Father Mignon was approached by the Mother Superior Jeanne des Anges (Joan of the Angels) for help.

Figure 23: *Urbain Grandier, who was convicted and executed as a result of the Loudun possessions*

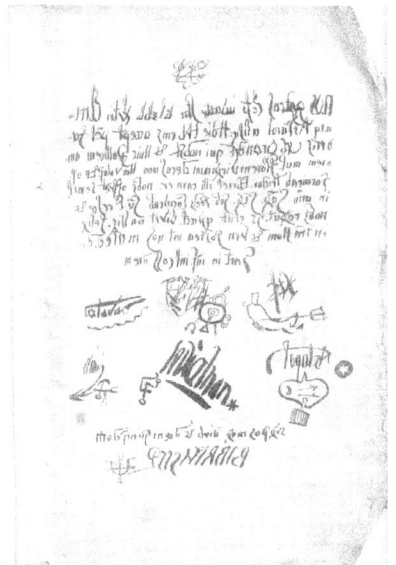

Figure 24: *Urbain Grandier's alleged diabolical pact*

According to the first story, Father Mignon readily persuaded the Mother Superior, Jeanne des Anges, and another nun to comply. They would claim that Father Grandier had bewitched them, falling into fits and convulsions, often holding their breath and speaking in tongues.

The second story claims that Jeanne had illicit dreams about Father Grandier, who appeared to her as a radiant angel. As an angel, he enticed her to sexual acts, causing her to rave loudly at night. Jeanne suffered flagellation and did penance for the night-time disturbances, but she was no less troubled and soon it was found that other nuns were being haunted by hallucinations and vulgar dreams. It was then, this version claims, that Mother Superior Jeanne des Anges called for Father Mignon to hear her confession and purge the convent of demons.

However it came about, Father Mignon and his aide, Father Pierre Barré, saw in the activity an opportunity to remove Grandier.

Fathers Mignon and Barré immediately proceeded to perform exorcisms on the possessed nuns. Several of the nuns, including Jeanne des Anges, suffered violent convulsions during the procedure, shrieking and making sexual motions toward the priests. Following the lead of Jeanne des Anges, many of the nuns reported illicit dreams. The accusers would suddenly bark, scream, blaspheme, and contort their bodies. During the exorcisms, Jeanne swore that she and the other nuns were possessed by two demons named Asmodeus and Zebulun. These demons were sent to the nuns when Father Grandier tossed a bouquet of roses over the convent walls.

Nearby and realizing the danger he was in, Father Grandier pleaded with the bailiff of Loudun to isolate the nuns; the bailiff's orders were ignored, and the exorcisms and denouncements continued. Desperate, Grandier wrote to the Archbishop of Bordeaux, who sent his personal doctor to examine the nuns. No evidences of true possession were found, and the Archbishop ordered the exorcisms to cease on March 21, 1633. The nuns were sequestered in their cells.

Having failed to remove Grandier, his contemporaries continued their efforts in earnest. One of these was Jean de Laubardemont, a relative of Jeanne des Anges' and favored by the powerful Cardinal Richelieu. Laubardemont and a Capuchin monk, Tranquille, visited the Cardinal with news of the unsuccessful exorcisms and added further evidence against Grandier by providing a copy of a libelous satire Grandier had written about Richelieu. Aware that a relative of his, Sister Claire, was in the Loudun convent, Richelieu asserted his power and organized the Royal Commission to arrest and investigate Grandier as a witch. Laubardemont was appointed head of the commission.

Public exorcisms at Loudun

When exorcisms resumed at Loudun, they were led by the expert exorcists Capuchin Father Tranquille, Franciscan Father Lactance, and Jesuit Father Jean-Joseph Surin, and they were held publicly; up to 7,000 spectators attended. The priests employed dramatic commands, threats, and rituals to both direct and encourage the nuns in their accusations against Grandier.

Adding to the hysteria prompted by the public exorcisms were the stories told by both nuns and Father Grandier's former lovers. As in both the Louviers possessions and the Aix-en-Provence possessions, the claims made against Grandier were overtly sexual and showed visible physical responses. Because they were public and dramatic, the citizens of Loudun and surrounding areas were set against Grandier.

In addition to the dreams that Jeanne des Anges and other nuns had related, Jeanne added a third demon to the array of possessors afflicting the nuns: Isacaron, the devil of debauchery. After admitting to this third demon possessor, Jeanne went through a psychosomatic pregnancy. In all, Jeanne and the other nuns claimed to be possessed by a multitude of demons: Asmodeus, Zabulon, Isacaaron, Astaroth, Gresil, Amand, Leviatom, Behemot, Beherie, Easas, Celsus, Acaos, Cedon, Naphthalim, Cham, Ureil and Achas.

In an effort to clear his name, Father Grandier performed an exorcism on the nuns himself. He spoke to the nuns in Greek, testing their knowledge of languages previously unknown to them (a sure sign of possession). The nuns had been coached, and responded that they had been ordered in their pact to never use Greek.

In another exorcism, performed by Father Gault, the priest obtained a promise from the demon Asmodeus to leave one of the nuns he was possessing. Later, a devil's pact allegedly written between the Devil and Grandier was presented to the court. In this pact, stolen from Lucifer's cabinet of pacts by Asmodeus himself, was signed in blood by Grandier and various demons. Asmodeus had apparently written out the same promise he'd given to Father Gault on this pact:

> I promise that when leaving this creature, I will make a slit below her heart as long as a pin, that this slit will pierce her shirt, bodice and cloth which will be bloody. And tomorrow, on the twentieth of May at five in the afternoon of Saturday, I promise that the demons Gresil and Amand will make their opening in the same way, but a little smaller - and I approve the promises made by Leviatam, Behemot, Beherie with their companions to sign, when leaving, the register of the church of St. Croix! Given the nineteenth of May 1629.

Later historians would prove that this note was written in Jeanne des Anges' hand.Wikipedia:Citation needed An image of the pact is presented at the top of this article.

Torture at Loudun

On December 7, 1633, Father Grandier was put in prison at the Castle of Angers. His body was shaved and a successful search for devil's marks was made by inquisitors. Protests by Dr. Fourneau, the physician who prepared Grandier for torture, and the apothecary from Poitiers were ignored. These protests claimed the inspection was a hoax, and stated that no such marks had been found.

Nicholas Aubin's 1693 *The Cheats and Illusions of Romish Priest and Exorcists Discovered in the History of the Devils of Loudun* describes what happened next:

> *They sent for Mannouri the surgeon, one of [Grandier's] enemies, and the most unmerciful of them all; when he [came] into the chamber, they stripped Grandier stark naked, blinded his eyes, shaved him every where, and Mannouri began to search him. When he would persuade them that the parts of his body which had been marked by the Devil were insensible, he turned that end of the probe which was round, and he guided it in such a manner, that not being able to enter into the flesh, nor to make much impression, it was pushed back into the palm of his hand; the patient did not then cry out, because he felt no pain; but when the barbarous surgeon would make them see that the other parts of his body were very sensible, he turned the probe at the other end, which was very sharp pointed, and thrust it to the very bone; and then the abundance of people [outside] heard complaints so bitter, and cries so piercing, that they [were] moved...to the heart*

Other people spoke in Grandier's defense, even some of the possessed nuns proclaimed his innocence. Laubardemont, fulfilling his duty to convict Grandier, explained that the nuns' reactions were a ploy by Satan to save Grandier. Jeanne des Anges appeared in court with a noose tied around her neck, violently stating that she would hang herself if she could not recant her earlier lies. All defenses were ignored, and some defense witnesses were pressured to keep silent. Publicly, Laubardemont announced that any citizens who testified in favour of Grandier would be arrested as traitors to the King and have their possessions confiscated. Many of these witnesses fled France.

While the defense witnesses were forced to flee, 72 witnesses swore evidence against Grandier, who was denied the normal procedure of trial by a secular court. Had he been tried by secular court, Grandier could have appealed to the Parliament of Paris. Instead, Richelieu's committee took charge of the legal proceedings.

Grandier's trial took place in Loudun itself, and he was closely imprisoned in the converted attic of a house there for the duration of it.

Nearly a year later, August 18, 1634, the Royal Commission found Grandier guilty of all counts against him and passed sentence - Grandier would be burned alive at the stake:

> We have ordered and do order the said Urbain Grandier duly tried and convicted of the crime of magic, maleficia, and of causing demoniacal possession of several Ursuline nuns of this town of Loudun, as well as of other secular women, together with other charges and crimes resulting therefrom. For atonement of which, we have condemned and do condemn the said Grandier to make amende honorable, his head bare, a rope round his neck, holding in his hand a burning taper weighing two pounds, before the principal door of the church of St. Pierre-du-Marché, and before that of St. Ursula of this town. There on his knees, to ask pardon of God, the King, and the law; this done, he is to be taken to the public square of St. Croix, and fastened to a stake on a scaffold, which shall be erected on the said place for this purpose, and there to be burned alive...and his ashes scattered to the wind. We have ordered and so do order that each and every article of his moveable property be acquired and confiscated by the King; the sum of 500 livres first being taken for buying a bronze plaque on which will be engraved the abstract of this present trial, to be set up in a prominent spot in the said church of the Ursulines, to remain there for all eternity. And before proceeding to the execution of the present sentence, we order the said Grandier to be submitted to the first and last degrees of torture, concerning his accomplices.

All details of the sentence were carried out.

Torture was a commonplace effort to extract confessions from accused witches during the seventeenth century, clearly recommended in the *Malleus Maleficarum*. Grandier was put to preliminary torture almost immediately after sentence was passed upon him. Most accused witches immediately confessed, telling their torturers exactly what they wanted to hear. Father Grandier never confessed, maintaining his innocence even under the most severe forms of torture. The method of torture used was the Brodequins, or Boot, which consisted of a total of sixteen to eighteen wedges driven between planks strongly bound to his legs, designed to slowly break the bones. He refused to name any accomplices, which drove Father Tranquille to break both Grandier's legs.

Burning at Loudun

Father Grandier was promised that he could have the chance to speak before he was executed, making a last statement, and that he would be hanged before the burning, an act of mercy. From the scaffold Grandier attempted to address the crowd, but the monks threw large quantities of holy water in his face so that his last words could not be heard. Then, according to historian Robert Rapley, exorcist Lactance caused the execution to deviate from the planned course of action—enraged by taunting from the crowd that gathered for the execution, Lactance lit the funeral pyre before Grandier could be hanged, leaving him to be burned alive.

The possessions failed to stop after Father Grandier's execution; as a result, public exorcisms continued. In his summary of the Loudun possessions, author Moshe Sluhovsky reports that these displays continued until 1637, three years after Grandier's death: "[t]he last departing demons left clear signs of their exit from her [Jeanne des Anges, the mother superior of the community] body, when the names Joseph and Mary miraculously appeared inscribed on des Anges's left arm." Allegedly, the Duchess d'Aiguillon, niece to Cardinal Richelieu, reported the fraud to her uncle.Wikipedia:Citation needed Having achieved his original goal, Richelieu terminated the investigations into the events at Loudun.Wikipedia:Citation needed

SomeWikipedia:Manual of Style/Words to watch#Unsupported attributions claim that it was actually Jeanne des Anges who had the public exorcisms stopped. Jeanne allegedly had a vision that she would be freed from the Devil if she made a pilgrimage to the tomb of Saint Francis de Sales. She went to Annecy, then visited Cardinal Richelieu and King Louis XIII in 1638; the demons were apparently gone.

Jeanne des Anges remained convinced of her own saintliness until she died in 1665.Wikipedia:Citation needed

Post historical analysis and criticism

In post analysis studies, Augustin Calmet, among others, has compared this case to the pretended possession of Martha Broissier (1578), a case which garnered a great deal of attention in its day. This comparison is based in part on the circumstances surrounding the incidents as well as the examinations of the possessions in question, all of which indicate pretended possessions, in contrast to cases considered more legitimate such as the possession of Mademoiselle Elizabeth de Ranfaing (1621). In his treatise, Calmet states that the causes of the injustice committed at Loudun were a mixture of political ambition, the need for attention, and a basic desire to dispose of political opponents. Calmet places the blame for the tragedy in Loudun with Cardinal Richelieu, chief minister of Louis XIII, and his goal of ruining Urbain Grandier, the Cure of Loudun.

Grandier became an enemy of Cardinal Richelieu when a libelous satire attributed to Grandier was anonymously published in 1618. However, his fate was likely sealed through obstructing the Cardinal's plan to demolish Loudun's fortifications, including the Castle of Loudon. The demolition, to be overseen by Jean de Laubardemont, was part of Richelieu's program of eliminating Huguenot strongholds by destroying local fortifications. The success of this mission would help cement the Cardinal's power both within the Church and within France.Wikipedia:Citation needed

Both Protestant (Huguenot) and Catholic residents of Loudun were against the removal of their battlements, which would have left them unprotected against mercenary armies. Grandier cited the King's promise that Loudun's walls would not be destroyed, successfully preventing Laubardemont from demolishing the fortifications. Laubardemont promptly reported back to Richelieu with an account of the failed exorcisms, the libelous satire, and Grandier's obstruction of Richelieu's plans, thus setting the tragedy in Loudun and Grandier's demise in motion.Wikipedia:Citation needed

Richelieu's strategy for destroying Grandier brought with it an added benefit for the Catholic Church: conversions. Many of the Protestant townspeople converted to Catholicism as a result of the public exorcisms, further eroding any Huguenot sentiment in the region.Wikipedia:Citation needed

Media

- The 1949 book titled *Drömmar om rosor och eld* by the Swedish author Eyvind Johnson tells the story of the trial of Urbain Grandier, priest of the town who was tortured and burned at the stake in 1634. He was accused of being in league with the Devil and having seduced an entire convent of nuns.
- The 1952 book titled *The Devils of Loudun* by Aldous Huxley tells the same story.
- John Whiting's 1961 theatre play *The Devils (play)*, commissioned by Sir Peter Hall for the Royal Shakespeare Company, was based on Aldous Huxley's novel.
- Krzysztof Penderecki's 1969 opera *The Devils of Loudun* (*Die Teufel von Loudun*), which premiered at the Hamburg State Opera, was based on Huxley's novel and Whiting's play.
- Ken Russell's 1971 film *The Devils* was based on Huxley's novel and Whiting's play.

External references

- Bodin, Jean. *The Witches and the Law. Witchcraft in Europe 1100-1700: A Documentary History.* Ed. Alan C. Kors & Edward Peters. Philadelphia: University of Pennsylvania Press. 1991.
- de Certeau, Michel. *The Possession at Loudun.* University of Chicago Press. 2000. ISBN 0-226-10034-0, ISBN 978-0-226-10034-0.
- Dumas, Alexander. *Urbain Grandier, Celebrated Crimes* - Available on Wikisource
- Sidky, H. Witchcraft, Lycanthropy, Drugs, and Disease: An Anthropological Study of the European Witch-Hunts[95]. New York: Peter Lang Publishing, Inc. 1997.

Anneliese Michel

Anneliese Michel	
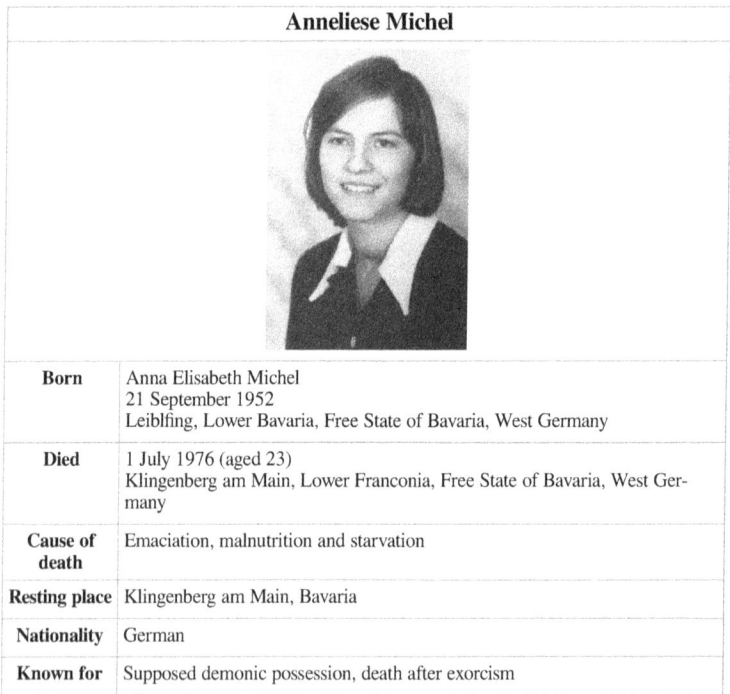	
Born	Anna Elisabeth Michel 21 September 1952 Leiblfing, Lower Bavaria, Free State of Bavaria, West Germany
Died	1 July 1976 (aged 23) Klingenberg am Main, Lower Franconia, Free State of Bavaria, West Germany
Cause of death	Emaciation, malnutrition and starvation
Resting place	Klingenberg am Main, Bavaria
Nationality	German
Known for	Supposed demonic possession, death after exorcism

Anna Elisabeth "Anneliese" Michel [ˈanəˌliːzə ˈmɪçl̩] (21 September 1952 – 1 July 1976) was a German woman who underwent Catholic exorcism rites during the year before her death. She was diagnosed with epileptic psychosis (temporal lobe epilepsy) and had a history of psychiatric treatment, which was overall not effective.

When Michel was sixteen, she experienced a seizure and was diagnosed with psychosis caused by temporal lobe epilepsy. Shortly thereafter, she was diagnosed with depression and was treated at a psychiatric hospital. By the time she was twenty, she had become intolerant of various religious objects and began to hear voices. Her condition worsened despite medication, and she became suicidal, also displaying other symptoms, for which she took medication as well. After taking psychiatric medications for five years failed to improve her symptoms, Michel and her family became convinced she was possessed by a demon. As a result, her family appealed to the Catholic Church for an exorcism. While rejected at first, after much hesitation, two priests got permission from the local bishop in 1975. Anneliese Michel stopped eating food and died due to malnourishment and dehydration. Michel's parents and the two Roman Catholic priests were found guilty of negligent homicide and were sentenced to six months in jail (reduced to three years of probation), as well as a fine.

The 2005 film *The Exorcism of Emily Rose* is based on her story.

Early life

Born as Anna Elisabeth Michel on 21 September 1952 in Leiblfing, Bavaria, West Germany, to a Roman Catholic family, Michel was brought up along with three sisters by her parents, Josef and Anna. She was religious and went to Mass twice a week. When she was sixteen, she suffered a severe convulsion and was diagnosed with temporal lobe epilepsy. In 1973, Michel graduated and joined the University of Würzburg. Her classmates later described her as "withdrawn and very religious".

Psychiatric treatment

In June 1970, Michel suffered a third seizure at the psychiatric hospital where she had been staying. She was prescribed anti-convulsion drugs for the first time, including Dilantin, which did not alleviate the problem. She began describing seeing "devil faces" at various times of the day. That same month, she was prescribed another drug, Aolept, which is similar to chlorpromazine and is used in the treatment of various psychoses including schizophrenia, disturbed behavior and delusions. By 1973, she suffered from depression and began hallucinating while praying, and complained about hearing voices telling her that she was "damned" and would "rot in hell". Michel's treatment in a psychiatric hospital did not improve her health and her depression worsened. Long term treatment did not help either, and she grew increasingly frustrated with the medical intervention, taking pharmacological drugs for five years. She began to attribute it to demonic possession. Michel became intolerant of Christian sacred places and objects, such as the crucifix.

Michel went to San Damiano with a family friend who regularly organized Christian pilgrimages.[96] Her escort concluded that she was suffering from demonic possession because she was unable to walk past a crucifix and refused to drink the water of a Christian holy spring: <templatestyles src="Template:Quote/styles.css"/>

> Anneliese told me—and Frau Hein confirmed this—that she was unable to enter the shrine. She approached it with the greatest hesitation, then said that the soil burned like fire and she simply could not stand it. She then walked around the shrine in a wide arc and tried to approach it from the back. She looked at the people who were kneeling in the area surrounding the little garden, and it seemed to her that while praying they were gnashing their teeth. She got as far as the edge of the little garden, then she had to turn back. Coming from the front again, she had to avert her glance from the picture of Christ [in the chapel of the house]. She made it several times to the garden, but could not get past it. She also noted that she could no longer look at medals or pictures of saints; they sparkled so immensely that she could not stand it. —Father Alt

Both she and her family, as well as her community, became convinced and consulted several priests, asking for an exorcism. The priests declined, recommended the continuation of medical treatment, and informed the family that exorcisms required the bishop's permission. In the Catholic Church, official approval for an exorcism is given when the person strictly meets the set criteria, then they are considered to be suffering from possession (*infestatio*) and under demonic control. Intense dislike for religious objects and "supernatural powers" are some of the first indications. Michel worsened physically and displayed aggression, self-injury, drank her own urine and ate insects. In November 1973, Michel started her treatment with Tegretol, an anti-seizure drug and mood stabilizer. She was prescribed anti-psychotic drugs during the course of the religious rites and took them frequently until some time before her death.

Exorcism and death

The priest Ernst Alt, whom they met, on seeing her declared that "she didn't look like an epileptic" and that he did not see her having seizures. Alt believed she was suffering from demonic possession and urged the local bishop to allow an exorcism. In a letter to Alt in 1975, Michel wrote, "I am nothing; everything about me is vanity. What should I do? I have to improve. You pray for

Figure 25: *Bishop Josef Stangl (May 1959) who approved the exorcism ordering total secrecy*

me" and also once told him, "I want to suffer for other people...but this is so cruel". In September of the same year, Bishop Josef Stangl granted the priest Arnold Renz permission to exorcise according to the *Rituale Romanum of 1614*, but ordered total secrecy.[97]</ref> Renz performed the first session on 24 September. Michel began talking increasingly about "dying to atone for the wayward youth of the day and the apostate priests of the modern church", and she refused to eat towards the end. At this point, her parents stopped consulting doctors on her request and relied solely on the exorcism rites. 67 exorcism sessions; one or two each week, lasting up to four hours, were performed over about ten months in 1975–1976.

On 1 July 1976, Michel died in her home. The autopsy report stated the cause was malnutrition and dehydration due to being in a semi-starvation state for almost a year while the rites of exorcism were performed. She weighed 30 kilograms (68 pounds), suffering broken knees due to continuous genuflections. She was unable to move without assistance, and was reported to have contracted pneumonia.

Prosecution

After an investigation, the state prosecutor maintained that Michel's death could have been prevented even one week before she died.

In 1976, the state charged Michel's parents and priests Ernst Alt and Arnold Renz with negligent homicide. During the case Michel's body was exhumed and tapes were played to the court of the exorcisms over the eleven months which led to her death. The parents were defended by Erich Schmidt-Leichner; their lawyers were sponsored by the Church. The state recommended that no involved parties be jailed; instead, the recommended sentence for the priests was a fine, while the prosecution concluded that the parents should be exempt from punishment as they had "suffered enough", which is a criterion in German penal law, cf. § 60 StGB.

Trial

The trial started on 30 March 1978 in the district court and drew intense interest. Before the court, doctors testified that Michel was not possessed, stating that this was a psychological effect because of her strict religious upbringing and her epilepsy, but the doctor Richard Roth, who was asked for medical help by Alt, allegedly told her during the exorcism, that "there is no injection against the devil, Anneliese". Schmidt-Leichner said that the exorcism was legal and that the German constitution protected citizens in the unrestricted exercise of their religious beliefs. The defense played tapes recorded at the exorcism sessions, sometimes featuring what was claimed to be "demons arguing", to assert their claim that Michel was possessed. Both priests said the demons identified themselves as Lucifer, Cain, Judas Iscariot, Hitler, and Nero among others; they further said that she was finally freed because of the exorcism just before her death.

The bishop said that he was not aware of her alarming health condition when he approved of the exorcism and did not testify. The accused were found guilty of manslaughter resulting from negligence and were sentenced to six months in jail (which was later suspended) and three years of probation. It was a far lighter sentence than anticipated, but it was more than requested by the prosecution, who had asked that the priests only be fined and that the parents be found guilty but not punished. The Church approving such an old fashioned exorcism rite drew public and media attention. According to John M. Duffey, the case was a misidentification of mental illness.

Figure 26: *Michel's gravestone. Her grave became a place of pilgrimage.*

Exhumation and aftermath

After the trial, the parents asked the authorities for permission to exhume the remains of their daughter. The official reason presented by the parents to authorities was that Michel had been buried in undue hurry in a cheap coffin. Almost two years after the burial, on 25 February 1978, her remains were replaced in a new oak coffin lined with tin. The official reports state that the body bore the signs of consistent deterioration. The accused exorcists were discouraged from seeing the remains of Michel. Arnold Renz later stated that he had been prevented from entering the mortuary. The church changed its position stating she was mentally ill, not possessed. Her grave became and remains a pilgrimage site.

Ulrich Niemann, a Jesuit priest, doctor, and psychiatrist, whom priests call in exorcism cases, told *The Washington Post* in 2005, "As a doctor, I say there is no such thing as possession... In my view, these patients are mentally ill. I pray with them, but that alone doesn't help. You have to deal with them as a psychiatrist. But at the same time, when the patient comes from Eastern Europe and believes that he's been impaired by evil, it would be a mistake to ignore his belief system." Niemann further said that he does not think he is an exorcist and does not perform the Roman ritual of 1614. Academic Heike

Schwarz says the Michel case showed demonic possession as a variation of multiple personality disorder (now known as dissociative identity disorder).

The number of officially sanctioned exorcisms decreased in Germany due to this case, in spite of Pope Benedict XVI's support for wider use of it compared to Pope John Paul II, who in 1999 made the rules stricter, involving only rare cases.

In 2013, a fire broke out in the house where Anneliese Michel lived, and, although the local police said it was a case of arson, some locals attributed it to the exorcism case.

In popular culture

- Three films, *The Exorcism of Emily Rose* (which focuses on the court case and not the exorcism), *Requiem* and *Anneliese: The Exorcist Tapes*, are loosely based on Michel's story.
- First Issue, the debut album from John Lydon's post Sex Pistols band Public Image Ltd contains the song 'Annalisa', about the case.[98]
- "The Chilling Exorcism of Anneliese Michel", released on 14 November 2016, was episode 4 of season 1 of BuzzFeed web series, *BuzzFeed Unsolved: Supernatural* in which the case and theories surrounding it were discussed.
- The case and its history was also covered in *Case 11: Anneliese Michel*, a March 2016 episode of the Casefile True Crime Podcast.

Further reading

- Goodman, Felicitas D. (1988). *How about Demons?: Possession and Exorcism in the Modern World*. Indianapolis: Indiana University Press. ISBN 0-253-32856-X.
- Felicitas D. Goodman (1 November 2005). *The Exorcism of Anneliese Michel*[99]. Resource Publications (OR). ISBN 978-1-59752-432-2.
- Getler, Micheal. "Cries of a Woman Possessed : German Court Hears Tapes in Exorcism Death Trial" in *The Washington Post* (21 April 1978)

External links

- Casefile True Crime Podcast - Case 11: Anneliese Michel[100] - 19 March 2016
- Anneliese Michel[101] at Find a Grave
- Dunning, Brian (8 March 2011). "Skeptoid #248: The Exorcism of Anneliese"[102]. *Skeptoid*. Retrieved 22 June 2017.

Martha Brossier

Martha Brossier	
Born	1556 Romorantin-Lanthenay, France
Other names	Martha Broissier, Madam Brossier, Marthe Brossier

Martha Brossier (1556- d. after 1578) was a French woman, infamous for feigning demonic possession at the age of 22.[103] The fraud was discovered by Charles Miron, bishop of either the Diocese of Angers or the Diocese of Orléans. According to Augustin Calmet, Martha, the daughter of a weaver in Romorantin, claimed to have been demonically possessed, drawing considerable notoriety. Her case of demonic possession is often cited by theological historians along with the Loudun possessions because both cases consist of notorious accounts of apparent demonic possession which are now presumed to have been fraudulent.[104]

Daemonic torment

The maladies from which she was recorded to suffer included an extreme shortness of breath, the ability to stick out her tongue unreasonably far, and the gnashing of her teeth. She would writhe and move her mouth as if she had convulsions while contorting her face, rolling her eyes and appearing to show deep vexation and torment. She would also contort her body parts. A rumbling noise was heard from the area of her spleen under her short ribs on her left side, causing her left thigh to spasm. She often spoke in a violent and roaring voice. She was recorded to have laid flat on her back and skip with her body, being able to span the distance from the altar to the door of a great chapel in four or five lifts, which onlookers described as giving an impression of her being dragged or lifted, presumably by demons. During her demonic fits, she was able to endure pin pricks to her hands and neck with limited bleeding. She was also able to speak with her mouth shut, often speaking English and Greek in fluency.

Discovery

Charles Miron discovered the fraud by making her drink holy water under the guise of normal water. He also had the exorcists present her with a key wrapped up in red silk (stating that the silk contained a relic of the 'true cross') and recite various verses from Virgil, which Martha Broisser's demon took for exorcism rites. As both the presence of the wrapped key and the recital of lines from Virgil agitated her immensely, the fraud became clear. Henri de Gondi, Cardinal Bishop of Paris, had her examined by five members of his faculty. Three were of the opinion that she was an impostor with little indication of malady. The Parliament nominated eleven physicians who all unanimously reported that there was nothing demonic in the matter,[105] suggesting that she used the physical strength of her stomach and breast to speak with her mouth shut.[106]

Notes

- Calmet, Augustin (1751). *Treatise on the Apparitions of Spirits and on Vampires or Revenants: of Hungary, Moravia, et al. The Complete Volumes I & II. 2015.* ISBN 1-5331-4568-7.
- Bernard, Richard (1627). *A Guide to Grand-Jury Men: In Modern English. 2017.* ISBN 1542697077.

Further reading

- Abraham Hartwell (1599). *A True Discourse Upon the Matter of Martha Brossier of Romorantin, pretended to be possessed by a Devil. 2018.* ISBN 1987654439.

Appendix

References

[1] //en.wikipedia.org/w/index.php?title=Template:Paranormal&action=edit
[2] Mohr, M. D., & Royal, K. D. (2012). "Investigating the Practice of Christian Exorcism and the Methods Used to Cast out Demons", Journal of Christian Ministry, 4, p. 35. Available at: http://journalofchristianministry.org/article/view/10287/7073.
[3] Malachi M. (1976) Hostage to the Devil: the possession and exorcism of five living Americans. San Francisco, Harpercollins p. 462
[4] http://cmje.usc.edu/religious-texts/hadith/bukhari/076-sbt.php#008.076.479
[5] Josephus, "B. J." vii. 6, § 3 http://www.earlyjewishwritings.com/text/josephus/war7.html; Sanh. 65b.
[6] http://taoist-sorcery.blogspot.com/2012/08/taoist-exorcism-by-taoist-master.html
[7] http://web.stanford.edu/group/hopes/cgi-bin/hopes_test/exorcism-and-mental-illness-across-different-cultures/
[8] http://www.patheos.com/Library/Taoism/Ritual-Worship-Devotion-Symbolism/Rites-and-Ceremonies?offset=1&max=1
[9] Henderson, J. (1981). *Exorcism and Possession in Psychotherapy Practice*. Canadian Journal of Psychiatry 27: 129–34.
[10] Maniam, T. (1987). *Exorcism and Psychiatric Illness: Two Case Reports*. Medical Journal of Malaysia. 42: 317–19.
[11] Pfeifer, S. (1994). *Belief in demons and exorcism in psychiatric patients in Switzerland*. British Journal of Medical Psychology 4 247–58.
[12] Beyerstein, Barry L. (1995). *Dissociative States: Possession and Exorcism*. In Gordon Stein (ed.). *The Encyclopedia of the Paranormal*. Prometheus Books. pp. 544–52.
[13] Tajima-Pozo, K., Zambrano-Enriquez, D., de Anta, L., Moron, M., Carrasco, J., Lopez-Ibor, J., & Diaz-Marsa, M. (2011). "Practicing exorcism in schizophrenia" https://www.ncbi.nlm.nih.gov/pmc/articles/PMC3062860/. Case Reports.
[14] Ross, C. A., Schroeder, B. A. & Ness, L. (2013). *Dissociation and symptoms of culture-bound syndromes in North America: A preliminary study*. Journal of Trauma & Dissociation 14: 224–35.
[15] Noll, Richard. (2006). *The Encyclopedia of Schizophrenia and Other Psychotic Disorders*. Facts On File Inc. p. 129.
[16] Levack, Brian P. (1992). *Possession and Exorcism*. Routledge. p. 5.
[17] Radford, Benjamin. (2005). "Voice of Reason: Exorcisms, Fictional and Fatal" http://www.livescience.com/9321-voice-reason-exorcisms-fictional-fatal.html. LiveScience. "To the extent that exorcisms "work," it is primarily due to the power of suggestion and the placebo effect."
[18] Levack, Brian P. (1992). *Possession and Exorcism*. Routledge. p. 277.
[19] The Patient Is the Exorcist http://www.beliefnet.com/story/159/story_15928.html, an interview with M. Scott Peck by Laura Sheahen
[20]
[21] Silverman, W A. "Neurosurgical Exorcism." Paediatric and Perinatal Epidemiology, 15.2 (2001): 98–99.
[22] Gettis, Alan. "Psychotherapy as exorcism." Journal of Religion and Health 15.3 (1976): 188–90.
[23] 'Spiritual abuse': Christian thinktank warns of sharp rise in UK exorcisms https://www.theguardian.com/world/2017/jul/05/christian-thinktank-warns-of-rise-in-exorcisms-mental-health *The Guardian*
[24] Dali's gift to exorcist uncovered http://www.cathnews.com/news/510/72.php Catholic News 14 October 2005.
[25] Duffey, John M. (2011). *Lessons Learned: The Anneliese Michel Exorcism*.
[26] https://books.google.com/?id=U5IBXA4UpT0C&dq=isbn:1421265311
[27] https://www.ncbi.nlm.nih.gov/pmc/articles/PMC3062860/

[28] https://www.ncbi.nlm.nih.gov/pmc/articles/PMC2495148/
[29] http://www.livescience.com/27727-exorcism-facts-and-fiction.html
[30] https://web.archive.org/web/20101224103059/http://www.audiosancto.org/sermon/20081007-An-Evening-with-an-Exorcist.html
[31] http://esorcismi.altervista.org/
[32] https://web.archive.org/web/20061213075345/http://images.dailykos.com/images/jindal.pdf
[33] http://jewishencyclopedia.com/view.jsp?artid=553&letter=E&search=Exorcism
[34] https://web.archive.org/web/20070108032631/http://www.cofe-worcester.org.uk/work_of_the_diocese/chaplaincy_deliverance.php
[35] http://www.goarch.org/ourfaith/ourfaith7079
[36] http://www.catholicdoors.com/prayers/latin/latin040.htm
[37] Mohr, M. D., & Royal, K. D. (2012). "Investigating the Practice of Christian Exorcism and the Methods Used to Cast out Demons", Journal of Christian Ministry, 4, p. 35. Available at: http://journalofchristianministry.org/article/view/10287/7073.
[38] Malachi M. (1976) Hostage to the Devil: the possession and exorcism of five living Americans. San Francisco, Harpercollins p.462
[39] ,; , ,
[40] JewishEncyclopedia.com - JESUS OF NAZARETH http://jewishencyclopedia.com/view.jsp?artid=254&letter=J&search=jesus%20casting%20out%20demons#998
[41] "Concerning Exorcism", *Book of Occasional Services*, Church Publishing.
[42] Martin M. (1976) *Hostage to the Devil: The Possession and Exorcism of Five Contemporary Americans*. Harper San Francisco. Appendix one "The Roman Ritual of Exorcism" p.459
[43] THE ROMAN RITUAL Translated by PHILIP T. WELLER, S.T.D. http://www.ewtn.com/library/prayer/roman2.txt
[44] Amorth G. (1990) An Exorcist Tells His Story. tns. MacKenzie N. Ignatius Press: San Francisco. pp157-160
[45] Geleta, Amsalu Tadesse. " Case Study: Demonization and the Practice of Exorcism in Ethiopian Churches http://www.lausanne.org/all-documents/ethiopian-case-study.html ". Lausanne Committee for World Evangelization, Nairobi, August 2000.
[46] Poloma M. (1982) The Charismatic Movement: is there a new Pentecost? p97
[47] Cuneo M. (2001) American Exorcism: Expelling Demons in the Land of Plenty. Doubleday: New York. pp.111-128
[48] Poloma M. (1982) The Charismatic Movement: is there a new Pentecost? p60
[49] Cuneo M. (2001) American Exorcism: Expelling Demons in the Land of Plenty. Doubleday: New York. pp.118-119
[50] 'Johann Hari: The devilish church practice of exorcism' https://www.independent.co.uk/opinion/commentators/johann-hari/johann-hari-the-devilish-church-practice-of-exorcism-770658.html The Independent, 18 Jan. 2008
[51] "Priest 'made £3m from fake exorcisms'" https://www.telegraph.co.uk/news/worldnews/1583812/Priest-made-3m-from-fake-exorcisms.html *Telegraph* 3 April 2008
[52] http://www.nlc-bnc.ca/obj/s4/f2/dsk1/tape10/PQDD_0019/MQ45476.pdf
[53] https://web.archive.org/web/20070108032631/http://www.cofe-worcester.org.uk/work_of_the_diocese/chaplaincy_deliverance.php
[54] http://www.goarch.org/ourfaith/ourfaith7079
[55] Catechism of the Council of Trent (Dublin 1829), p. 310 https://archive.org/stream/thecatechismofth00donouoft/thecatechismofth00donouoft_djvu.txt
[56] Boudinhon, A. (1911). Minor Orders http://www.newadvent.org/cathen/10332b.htm in *The Catholic Encyclopedia*. New York: Robert Appleton Company. Retrieved May 21, 2014 from New Advent.
[57] Letter to Fabius, cited in Eusebius, Church History VI http://www.newadvent.org/fathers/250106.htm 43.11. Translated by Arthur Cushman McGiffert. From *Nicene and Post-Nicene Fathers*, Second Series, Vol. 1. Edited by Philip Schaff and Henry Wace. (Buffalo, New York: Christian Literature Publishing Co., 1890.) Revised and edited for New Advent by Kevin Knight.
[58] Toner, Patrick. "Exorcist" http://www.newadvent.org/cathen/05711a.htm *The Catholic Encyclopedia*. Vol. 5. New York: Robert Appleton Company, 1909. 21 May 2014 .

[59] Cyril of Jerusalem. Catechetical Lecture 20 http://www.newadvent.org/fathers/310120.htm (or *On The Mysteries*, Lecture 2). Translated by Edwin Hamilton Gifford. From *Nicene and Post-Nicene Fathers*, Second Series, Vol. 7. Edited by Philip Schaff and Henry Wace. (Buffalo, New York: Christian Literature Publishing Co., 1894.) Revised and edited for New Advent by Kevin Knight.

[60] Scannell, T. (1908). "Catechumen" http://www.newadvent.org/cathen/03430b.htm in *The Catholic Encyclopedia*. New York: Robert Appleton Company. Retrieved May 21, 2014 from New Advent.

[61] Toner, Patrick. (1909). "Exorcism" http://www.newadvent.org/cathen/05709a.htm in *The Catholic Encyclopedia*. New York: Robert Appleton Company. Retrieved May 21, 2014 from New Advent.

[62] Augustine of Hippo. *On Marriage and Concupiscence* (Book II) http://www.newadvent.org/fathers/15072.htm. Paragraph 50. Translated by Peter Holmes and Robert Ernest Wallis, and revised by Benjamin B. Warfield. From *Nicene and Post-Nicene Fathers*, First Series, Vol. 5. Edited by Philip Schaff. (Buffalo, New York: Christian Literature Publishing Co., 1887.) Revised and edited for New Advent by Kevin Knight.

[63] Paul VI. *Ministeria quaedam* http://www.vatican.va/holy_father/paul_vi/motu_proprio/documents/hf_p-vi_motu-proprio_19720815_ministeria-quaedam_lt.html, II: "The orders hitherto called minor are henceforth to be spoken of as 'ministries'."

[64] Constitutions of the Second Vatican Council: *Sacrosanctam Concilium* http://www.vatican.va/archive/hist_councils/ii_vatican_council/documents/vat-ii_const_19631204_sacrosanctum-concilium_en.html n. 64

[65] In the USA edition, at paragraphs 93A–93K, indicated as translations of 113-118 and 373.1-373.5 in the Latin original.

[66] USA edition, rubrics 98-101, translating Latin 103, 127-129, 212.

[67] USA rite, 300, translating Latin prayers 339 & 392.

[68] USA rite, 463 & 470, original material in English with no Latin antecedent.

[69] p.43 An Exorcist Tells His Story by Fr. Gabriele Amorth; Ignatius Press, San Francisco, 1999.

[70] Catechism of the Catholic Church, paragraph 1673

[71] Martin M. (1976) *Hostage to the Devil: The Possession and Exorcism of Five Contemporary Americans*. Harper San Francisco. Appendix one "The Roman Ritual of Exorcism" p.459

[72] THE ROMAN RITUAL Translated by PHILIP T. WELLER, S.T.D. http://www.ewtn.com/library/prayer/roman2.txt

[73] *The Rite*, by Matt Baglio; Doubleday, New York, 2009.

[74] http://www.mattbaglio.com

[75] http://content.time.com/time/nation/article/0,8599,1885372,00.html

[76] http://www.examiner.com/article/the-rite-by-matt-baglio-a-review

[77] http://catholicspotlight.com/545/cs125-matt-baglio-the-rite/

[78] http://www.archden.org/index.cfm/ID/9317

[79] http://www.usccb.org/prayer-and-worship/sacraments-and-sacramentals/sacramentals-blessings/exorcism.cfm

[80] http://www.catholicdoors.com/prayers/latin/latin040.htm

[81] http://exorcismus.org/what-is-an-exorcism/

[82] Joseph P. Laycock *Spirit Possession around the World: Possession, Communion, and Demon Expulsion across Cultures* ABC-CLIO 2015 page 166

[83] N. Ahmadi *Iranian Islam: The Concept of the Individual* Springer 1998 page 79

[84] 'Umar Sulaymān Ashqar *The World of the Jinn and Devils* Islamic Books 1998 page 204

[85] Moiz Ansari *Islam and the Paranormal: What Does Islam Says About the Supernatural in the Light of Qur'an, Sunnah And Hadith* iUniverse 2006 page 55

[86] Kelly Bulkeley, Kate Adams, Patricia M. Davis *Dreaming in Christianity and Islam: Culture, Conflict, and Creativity* Rutgers University Press 2009 page 148

[87] G. Hussein Rassool *Islamic Counselling: An Introduction to Theory and Practice* Routledge 2015 page 58

[88] Josef W. Meri *Medieval Islamic Civilization: An Encyclopedia* Routledge 2005 page 496

[89] http://cmje.usc.edu/religious-texts/hadith/bukhari/076-sbt.php#008.076.479

[90] http://duas.wiki-net.tk/Ruqya-treatment.php

[91] http://ruqyainlondon.com/article/evil-eye-and-envy-ayn
[92] http://www.howtobecomearaqi.com
[93] http://quod.lib.umich.edu/e/eebo/A07467.0001.001/1:4?rgn=div1;view=fulltext
[94] http://www.bestwebbuys.com/Man_Myth_and_Magic-ISBN_185435731X.html?isrc=b-search
[95] https://www.jstor.org/stable/2544763
[96] Interviews in "Satan lebt – Die Rückkehr des Exorzismus", 2006, wdr, Documentary by Helge Cramer.
[97] "In Nov '73, exorcism expert Jesuit priest Adolf Rodewyk examined Michel and recommended exorcism, which Stangl authorized in Sept '75."<ref>Annelise Michel was supposedly possessed by Satan. Craig R. Whitney (8 August 1976, Aschaffenburg (W Ger)). *The New York Times*, Page 10, Column 3 (103 words). Retrieved 11 May 2015.
[98] Chris Brazier: "The Danceable Solution" (Melody Maker, 28 October 1978)
[99] https://books.google.com/books?id=_DO9AAAACAAJ
[100] http://casefilepodcast.com/case-11-anneliese-michel/
[101] https://www.findagrave.com/memorial/11381816
[102] https://skeptoid.com/episodes/4248
[103] p. 22.
[104] p. 132.
[105] p. 132.
[106] p. 24.

Article Sources and Contributors

The sources listed for each article provide more detailed licensing information including the copyright status, the copyright owner, and the license conditions.

Exorcism *Source:* https://en.wikipedia.org/w/index.php?oldid=859461930 *License:* Creative Commons Attribution-Share Alike 3.0 *Contributors:* Ad Orientem, Allixpeeke, Animalparty, Anupam, Auric, BD2412, Batreeq, Bawb131, Bejnar, Bladesmuin, Brayan Jaimes, BrightR, Bronze2018, Bruce1ee, Caballero1967, Cannolis, Carlyoconnor, Carterpill, Chris the speller, ChrisGualtieri, ClarkAb, ClueBot NG, Cnephas, Coffeepusher, CommonsDelinker, Dirkbb, Donner60, Dontreader, DrAGONSOLDIER1234, Editor2020, Excirial, Faizi1997, Favonian, Finnusertop, Fuortu, GangofOne, Gilliam, Goblin Face, GoingBatty, Groyolo, Hafspajen, Hifrommike65, Hodgdon's secret garden, Htet Oo Lwin, I dream of horses, JC7V7DC5768, Jamesx12345, Jeraphine Gryphon, Jjmmff2015, John Link, Jonesey95, Josebarbosa, K6ka, KAMiKAZOW, KBH96, Kdroya2, Kendraalix944, KingAlanl, Leschnei, Library Guy, Lojbanist, Lord0fHats, MONGO, Magioladitis, ManKnowsInfinity, Mandarax, Mangoe, Marcocapelle, Mark Arsten, MatthewVanitas, Medlicense, MelbourneStar, Michipedian, Mike&Shannon123, Modysayed1, Mogism, MrBill3, Mysticalresearch, NeonCaki, Nova kitt the witch, OccultZone, Omnipaedista, Optimale, Orphan Wiki, Oshwah, Ostensibly1, Philip Trueman, Potenttomato, Proclamator, Proxima Centauri, Q6637p, Quebec99, RL0919, Rickymawnster, Rp2006, Rubym123, Ryn78, Serevix, Shane Cyrus, Solarra, Srich32977, Steeletrap, Tahc, Tenjan, Tgeorgescu, Thearjunpp, Theoreader, TwoTwoHello, Tyler RB Waldner, Wario-Man, Wiae, Wiki-uk, Xcuref1endx, Yolomaster101, 188 anonymous edits 1

Exorcism in Christianity *Source:* https://en.wikipedia.org/w/index.php?oldid=852576314 *License:* Creative Commons Attribution-Share Alike 3.0 *Contributors:* Alynna Kasmira, Amaury, Anupam, BD2412, Bejnar, BrightR, Callamachus, Carterpill, ClueBot NG, Colbey84, CommonsDelinker, DeCausa, Dsp13, Dusty777, Editor2020, Esoglou, Felovespiritfruit0333, Gareth Griffith-Jones, GoingBatty, Hazhk, Here2help, HiEv, Hmains, Jfhutson, JoeHebda, John Carter, Jonesey95, Jzsj, K6ka, Kdroya2, Khazar2, Lees1234, LovelyLillith, Lucifero4, Magioladitis, Mairi, Marcocapelle, Marek69, Matanya, Mysticalresearch, Ocaasi, R'n'B, Rrivera1977, Rubicon, Serols, Sjö, Theoreader, Thuateira, Tom.Reding, Topbanana, Widr, XVI Chancer, イザヤ, 55 anonymous edits 13

Minor exorcism in Christianity *Source:* https://en.wikipedia.org/w/index.php?oldid=818959559 *License:* Creative Commons Attribution-Share Alike 3.0 *Contributors:* Anupam, Bearcat, Bejnar, ClueBot NG, Colonies Chris, DuncanHill, DynamoDegsy, Gleyshon, John of Reading, Kamil10pl, Tom.Reding, TutterMouse, 1 anonymous edits 27

Exorcism in the Catholic Church *Source:* https://en.wikipedia.org/w/index.php?oldid=852576326 *License:* Creative Commons Attribution-Share Alike 3.0 *Contributors:* Alynna Kasmira, Anupam, BD2412, Bazonka, Bejnar, Bongwarrior, Carterpill, Chris the speller, ClueBot NG, Colbey84, CommonsDelinker, Dr Gangrene, Edinamic, Epicgenius, FWizard, François de Commines, Ginkgo100, GoingBatty, Gwen-chan, Hmainsbot1, Javert2113, Joefromrandb, John of Reading, Joseph A. Spadaro, Jsnwiki, KGirlTrucker81, Magioladitis, MikeLHenderson, Mjtheron, Mx. Granger, Niceguyedc, Nihiltres, Ninney, Omnipaedista, PhilSchabus, Prinsgezinde, R'n'B, RightCowLeftCoast, Rrivera1977, Slightsmile, Sock, Solarra, Stylteralmaldo, Surtsicna, There'sNoTime, Ugog Nizdast, WAvegetarian, Waddie96, Widr, Woohookitty, Xopher, Yorick77, Zackariaw, イザヤ, 120 anonymous edits 31

Exorcism in Islam *Source:* https://en.wikipedia.org/w/index.php?oldid=859275876 *License:* Creative Commons Attribution-Share Alike 3.0 *Contributors:* 7&6=thirteen, Admiral Caius, Al-Andalusi, Amal MR, Asif756, Batreeq, Brooksm12, Chintu6, ClueBot NG, Destroyer11623, Diannaa, DrRC, Gdominik100, GoodParaboè, Green&Yellow1, Gronk Oz, Hamzasiddiq, Holdoffhunger, Jackmcbarn, Johnstarlight72, Matt Fitzpatrick, Mr. Smart LION, Mx. Granger, Nadalbk, Pepperbeast, Pol098, Qarion, Rjwilmsi, Shafi (Abdalshafi) Ghwerien, Umairdr82, VenusFeuerFalle, WikiDan61, Xtremedood, بمان المامى, 28 anonymous edits 39

Ghosts in Tibetan culture *Source:* https://en.wikipedia.org/w/index.php?oldid=857583760 *License:* Creative Commons Attribution-Share Alike 3.0 *Contributors:* Anna Frodesiak, Aymatth2, Candleabracadabra, Dream of Nyx, Editor2020, Emir of Wikipedia, Emptymountains, Fixer88, Jmcgnh, Linespero, Moonsell, Randy Kryn, Rjwilmsi, Sandstein, Tarchunes, Truthsayer62, VictoriaGrayson, Welsh, 10 anonymous edits 45

Louvier possessions *Source:* https://en.wikipedia.org/w/index.php?oldid=844255170 *License:* Creative Commons Attribution-Share Alike 3.0 *Contributors:* 999〜enwiki, Aciram, Anupam, Asarelah, Bialosz, Dimadick, Ground Zero, Hmains, Jaraalbe, Lolaness, Makemi, Mark Ironie, Michael Devore, Silver starfish, 7 anonymous edits 49

Aix-en-Provence possessions *Source:* https://en.wikipedia.org/w/index.php?oldid=800739662 *License:* Creative Commons Attribution-Share Alike 3.0 *Contributors:* 999〜enwiki, Aciram, Alexandrathorn, Asarelah, Cangleesa, Cap'n Tightpants, Crystallina, CultureDrone, Dimadick, Edgeesa, FrigidNinja, Ian Pitchford, Ian.thomson, Jaraalbe, Jeraphine Gryphon, Lolaness, Magioladitis, Mark Ironie, Maudlin galore, Nlu, NoAamCom, Rich Farmbrough, Rjwilmsi, Ser Amantio di Nicolao, Shipsonty, Silver starfish, Squiddy, Underwaterbuffalo, Woubeauthrozboubleberry, 14 anonymous edits 52

Loudun possessions *Source:* https://en.wikipedia.org/w/index.php?oldid=853923477 *License:* Creative Commons Attribution-Share Alike 3.0 *Contributors:* 991joseph, 999〜enwiki, Aciram, Adam Bishop, Aegisrover, Ajpolino, All Scars, Anupam, Asarelah, Auric, Bgwhite, Brute nm, BryanG, Cabria, CanisRufus, Carina Keel, Casliber, Ccgrimm, Chienlit, ClueBot NG, DC Elliott, DE, Dimadick, Discworldian, Drmies, Eldamorie, Giraffedata, GoingBatty, Gyre, HamadaFanFFSM, Hampton11235, Ian.thomson, Igiffin, Ignoto, Improv, Iridescent, Jack1956, JackofOz, Jaraalbe, Jason Quinn, Jeepday, Johnnybna, Jossi, Kahtar, Lolaness, Lotje, Mark Ironie, Mboverload, Mezigue, Midnightblueowl, Mungo Shuntbox, Mysticalresearch, Philip Cross, Piposullivan, Po Mieczu, Portillo, Rbraunwa, Rjwilmsi, Sanya7901, Sfan00 IMG, Shindon Grasic, Squiddy, Starbox120862, Student7, TimBentley, Tony-TheTiger, Tripofmice, Underwaterbuffalo, Xandar, Xxanthippe, 59 anonymous edits 56

Anneliese Michel *Source:* https://en.wikipedia.org/w/index.php?oldid=858258616 *License:* Creative Commons Attribution-Share Alike 3.0 *Contributors:* 65HCA7, AAKSSH SWARNAKR, Abelmoschus Esculentus, AgeOfPlantageneet, AldezD, Americus55, Anonymous from the 21st century, Anti-CompositeNumber, Anupam, Auric, BabbaQ, Bapreme, Barerjamel, Belmontian, Bongwarrior, Buddy23Lee, CandyKittyGaming, Chief Red Eagle, Chrissymad, ClueBot NG, Cmr08, Commons fair use upload bot (usurped), CommonsDelinker, Crito10, DagosNavy, Danny.margerete.1972, DavidLeighEllis, Dl2000, Dolotta, Eaglizard, EamonnPKeane, Flyer22 Reborn, Fraggle81, Fram, GBRV, Gadget850, Gaute13, Gdallaire, Gene Wilson, GreekJonathanK, Gulumeemee, Hamreen, Ian.thomson, Jabberjaw, Jamesx12345, Javert2113, JeBonSer, Jeraphine Gryphon, Jim Michael, Jim1138, Joe Vitale 5, Keanu-Moowgliie, Keyosuke, KoshVorlon, Kpzthdl, KylieTastic, Lalmohan Babu, Lugia2453, Magicatthemovies, Marcocapelle, Materialscientist, Melonkelon, Mfield, Michipedian, MrBill3, Mswarner2016, Niet-0-leuk, Non-dropframe, Otherbackergroung, Opus 113, Oshwah, PaleoNeonate, Paul Barlow, Pewds-Bro12, PhilKnight, PlyrStar93, PohranicniStraze, Rides, Rosenzweig, Ryn78, Santiago Claudio, Sfthenerd, Simplexity22, Six words, Slightsmile, Soggagogga, Starkinson, SubSeven, Sugarbat, TransporterMan, Tucson Brown, Ugog Nizdast, Ukexpat, UnsungKing123, Waacstats, Waitalie Nat, WikiPlazzer, Wordsmythe123, Worldanthistory, Yamaguchi先生, Yintan, IΞXΣNIKA-888, 186 anonymous edits 64

Martha Brossier *Source:* https://en.wikipedia.org/w/index.php?oldid=842295777 *License:* Creative Commons Attribution-Share Alike 3.0 *Contributors:* Aciram, Alvin Seville, Editor2020, Giraffedata, John of Reading, Mysticalresearch, Postcard Cathy, Proclamator, Qetuth, 10 anonymous edits 71

Image Sources, Licenses and Contributors

The sources listed for each image provide more detailed licensing information including the copyright status, the copyright owner, and the license conditions.

Image *Source:* https://en.wikipedia.org/w/index.php?title=File:St._Francis_Borgia_Helping_a_Dying_Impenitent_by_Goya.jpg *License:* Public Domain *Contributors:* Balbo, Elisfkc, Escarlati, Evrik, Green Giant, Joanbanjo, Juiced lemon, Leyo, Mattes, Shakko, Tiberioclaudio99, Tremendo, Wst 1
Figure 1 *Source:* https://en.wikipedia.org/w/index.php?title=File:JesusCuresamute.gif *License:* Public Domain *Contributors:* Abraham, File Upload Bot (Magnus Manske), Jbarta, Jbribeiro1, OgreBot 2, Selket, Wst 2
Figure 2 *Source:* https://en.wikipedia.org/w/index.php?title=File:Ottava_di_San_Filippo_d'Agira_a_Limina_-_Province_of_Messina,_Sicily,_Italy_-_Sunday_19_May_2013.jpg *License:* Creative Commons Attribution-Sharealike 2.0 *Contributors:* fa.b 3
Figure 3 *Source:* https://en.wikipedia.org/w/index.php?title=File:Kashtbhanjan.jpg *License:* GNU Free Documentation License *Contributors:* Wheredevelsdare (talk) 4
Image *Source:* https://en.wikipedia.org/w/index.php?title=File:Wikisource-logo.svg *License:* Creative Commons Attribution-Sharealike 3.0 *Contributors:* ChrisiPK, Guillom, INeverCry, Jarekt, JuTa, Leyo, Lokal Profil, MichaelMaggs, NielsF, Rei-artur, Rocket000, Romaine, Steinsplitter 11
Figure 4 *Source:* https://en.wikipedia.org/w/index.php?title=File:JesusCuresamute.gif *License:* Public Domain *Contributors:* Abraham, File Upload Bot (Magnus Manske), Jbarta, Jbribeiro1, OgreBot 2, Selket, Wst 14
Figure 5 *Source:* https://en.wikipedia.org/w/index.php?title=File:St._Francis_Borgia_Helping_a_Dying_Impenitent_by_Goya.jpg *License:* Public Domain *Contributors:* Balbo, Elisfkc, Escarlati, Evrik, Green Giant, Joanbanjo, Juiced lemon, Leyo, Mattes, Shakko, Tiberioclaudio99, Tremendo, Wst 15
Figure 6 *Source:* https://en.wikipedia.org/w/index.php?title=File:Ottava_di_San_Filippo_d'Agira_a_Limina_-_Province_of_Messina,_Sicily,_Italy_-_Sunday_19_May_2013.jpg *License:* Creative Commons Attribution-Sharealike 2.0 *Contributors:* fa.b 17
Figure 7 *Source:* https://en.wikipedia.org/w/index.php?title=File:Folio_166r_-_The_Exorcism.jpg *License:* Public Domain *Contributors:* Cirt, Petrusbarbygere, Shakko, Skipjack, Un1c0s bot~commonswiki, Wst, 1 anonymous edits 23
Figure 8 *Source:* https://en.wikipedia.org/w/index.php?title=File:Folio_164r_-_The_Canaanite_Woman.jpg *License:* Public Domain *Contributors:* Bukk, Petrusbarbygere, Shakko, Un1c0s bot~commonswiki, Wst, 1 anonymous edits 23
Figure 9 *Source:* https://en.wikipedia.org/w/index.php?title=File:Healing_of_the_demon-possessed.jpg *License:* Public Domain *Contributors:* AndreasPraefcke, Geogast, JMCC1, Markus Mueller~commonswiki, Mbenoist, Nyttend, Shakko, Skipjack, Wst, Xoristzatziki, 2 anonymous edits .. 23
Figure 10 *Source:* https://en.wikipedia.org/w/index.php?title=File:Christus_heilt_einen_Besessenen.jpg *License:* Public Domain *Contributors:* Bwag, History2007, Lewenstein, Xenophon 24
Figure 11 *Source:* https://en.wikipedia.org/w/index.php?title=File:Sant_Apollinare_Nuovo_-_Healing_of_the_demon-possessed.jpg *License:* Public Domain *Contributors:* Batchheizer, DenghiùComm, Sailko, Testus, 1 anonymous edits 24
Figure 12 *Source:* https://en.wikipedia.org/w/index.php?title=File:Schnorr_von_Carolsfeld_Bibel_in_Bildern_1860_191.png *License:* Public Domain *Contributors:* McLeod, Primaler, 1 anonymous edits 25
Figure 13 *Source:* https://en.wikipedia.org/w/index.php?title=File:JesusCuresamute.gif *License:* Public Domain *Contributors:* Abraham, File Upload Bot (Magnus Manske), Jbarta, Jbribeiro1, OgreBot 2, Selket, Wst 25
Figure 14 *Source:* https://en.wikipedia.org/w/index.php?title=File:GiottoArezzo.jpg *License:* Public Domain *Contributors:* BotMultichill, DenghiùComm, Elya, G.dallorto, Mathiasrex, Sailko, 2 anonymous edits 26
Figure 15 *Source:* https://en.wikipedia.org/w/index.php?title=File:InfantBaptism.jpg *License:* GNU Free Documentation License *Contributors:* Farragutful, File Upload Bot (Magnus Manske), J 1982, Kelly, Nyttend, OgreBot 2 28
Image *Source:* https://en.wikipedia.org/w/index.php?title=File:PD-icon.svg *License:* Public Domain *Contributors:* Alex.muller, Anomie, Anonymous Dissident, CBM, Jo-Jo Eumerus, MBisanz, PBS, Quadell, Rocket000, Strangerer, Timotheus Canens, 1 anonymous edits 31
Figure 16 *Source:* https://en.wikipedia.org/w/index.php?title=File:St._Francis_Borgia_Helping_a_Dying_Impenitent_by_Goya.jpg *License:* Public Domain *Contributors:* Balbo, Elisfkc, Escarlati, Evrik, Green Giant, Joanbanjo, Juiced lemon, Leyo, Mattes, Shakko, Tiberioclaudio99, Tremendo, Wst 32
Figure 17 *Source:* https://en.wikipedia.org/w/index.php?title=File:Spinello_Aretino_Exorcism_of_St_Benedict.jpg *License:* Public Domain *Contributors:* SPINELLO ARETINO 34
Figure 18 *Source:* https://en.wikipedia.org/w/index.php?title=File:Ottava_di_San_Filippo_d'Agira_a_Limina_-_Province_of_Messina,_Sicily,_Italy_-_Sunday_19_May_2013.jpg *License:* Creative Commons Attribution-Sharealike 2.0 *Contributors:* fa.b 35
Figure 19 *Source:* https://en.wikipedia.org/w/index.php?title=File:Naskh_script_-_Qur'anic_verses.jpg *License:* Public Domain *Contributors:* Unknown Calligrapher 40
Figure 20 *Source:* https://en.wikipedia.org/w/index.php?title=File:Jinn_from_Ali_manuscript.jpg *License:* Public Domain *Contributors:* Lotje, Sherurcij, Tarih, 1 anonymous edits 43
Figure 21 *Source:* https://en.wikipedia.org/w/index.php?title=File:Gnam-khyi_nag-po1._Tibetaan_sa-bdag.jpg *License:* Creative Commons Attribution-Sharealike 3.0 *Contributors:* Dieter Schuh 46
Figure 22 *Source:* https://en.wikipedia.org/w/index.php?title=File:Ballard_Kadampa_Buddhist_Temple_interior_02.jpg *License:* GNU Free Documentation License *Contributors:* Joe Mabel 48
Figure 23 *Source:* https://en.wikipedia.org/w/index.php?title=File:Urbain_Grandier.jpg *License:* Public Domain *Contributors:* BeatrixBelibaste, Guise, Mu 57
Figure 24 *Source:* https://en.wikipedia.org/w/index.php?title=File:UrbainPact2.jpg *License:* Public Domain *Contributors:* Urbain Grandier ... 57
Image *Source:* https://en.wikipedia.org/w/index.php?title=File:Anneliese_Michel.jpg *Contributors:* - 64
Figure 25 *Source:* https://en.wikipedia.org/w/index.php?title=File:Bischof_josef_Stangl_Prozession_zur_Obernauer_Kapalle_1.5.1959.jpg *License:* Creative Commons Attribution-Sharealike 3.0,2.5,2.0,1.0 *Contributors:* Ekpah 67
Figure 26 *Source:* https://en.wikipedia.org/w/index.php?title=File:Gravestone_Anneliese_Michel.jpg *License:* Creative Commons Attribution-Sharealike 3.0 *Contributors:* User:Offenbacherjung 69

License

Creative Commons Attribution-Share Alike 3.0
//creativecommons.org/licenses/by-sa/3.0/

Index

Abbess, 56
Abbey, 49, 58
Abraham Hartwell, 10, 72
Adhan, 6, 41
Adolf Hitler, 68
A Guide to Grand-Jury Men, 72
Aix-en-Provence, 52
Aix-en-Provence possessions, 49, 51, **52**, 56, 59
Al-Baqara 255, 5, 41
Albert Mohler, 16
Aldous Huxley, 63
Alfred Richard Allinson, 52
Al-Jinn, 40
Alms, 20
Al-Muzzammil, 40
Altar, 49
Al-Tibb al-Nabawi, 39
Amende honorable, 61
Amulet, 2, 13
Angel, 2, 13
Anglican, 29
Anglican Church of Tanzania, 29
Anglican Communion, 29
Annecy, 62
Anneliese Michel, 9, 36, **64**
Anneliese: The Exorcist Tapes, 70
Anointing oil, 21
Antipsychotic, 66
Apostasy, 67
Apostle (Christian), 14, 18
Apostles Creed, 4
Apostolic Tradition, 28
Apothecary, 60
Appetite, 34
Arabic, 39
Arabic language, 39
Archangel, 2, 13
Archangel Michael, 4
Archbishop of Bordeaux, 58
Arezzo, 26
Armand Jean du Plessis, Cardinal Richelieu, 58
Asmodai, 59
Asmodeus, 56, 58

Astaroth, 59
Atharva Veda, 5
Auditory hallucination, 65
Augustin Calmet, 10, 62, 71
Augustine of Hippo, 28
Autopsy, 67

Bailiff, 58
Bantam Books, 36
Baptised, 27
Baptism, 4, 17, 18, 31
Baptist, 16
Bardo, 45
Barry Beyerstein, 10, 73
Basic Law for the Federal Republic of Germany, 68
Basil of Caesarea, 18
Basmala, 40
Bavaria, 65
Behemoth, 59
Bel-Nor, Missouri, 9
Benjamin Radford, 11, 73
Berkley Books, 36
Bhagavad Gita, 5
Bhagavata Purana, 5
Bhavacakra, 45
Bishop, 16, 65
Bishop of Poitiers, 56
Black magic, 5
Black Mass, 54
Blasphemy, 18, 19, 32, 49, 58
Blight, 18
Blood of Christ, 21
Bobby Jindal, 10
Book of Common Prayer, 29
Boot (torture), 61
Boy possessed by a demon, 23
Brahma, 5
Brian Dunning (author), 70
Brian P. Levack, 73
British Methodist Church, 21
Buda (folk religion), 21
Buddhism, 45
Burned at the stake, 56

BuzzFeed, 70
BuzzFeed Unsolved, 70

Cain and Abel, 68
Cannibalism, 53
Canon law (Catholic Church), 18, 32
Canons of Hippolytus, 28
Carbamazepine, 66
Cardinal (Catholicism), 58
Cardinal Richelieu, 63
Casefile True Crime Podcast, 70
Catechism of the Catholic Church, 10, 31
Catechist, 30
Catechumens, 28
Category:Paranormal, 1
Catholic Church, 31, 56, 65, 66
Catholic Encyclopedia, 11, 14, 27, 31, 37
Catholicism, 63
Catholic priests, 29
Celibacy, 56
Charismatic Movement, 22
Charles Miron, 71
Château dAngers, 60
Chlorpromazine, 65
Christ exorcising a mute, 26
Christ exorcising at sunset, 25
Christian Church, 2, 13, 27
Christian demonology, 2, 13
Christian denomination, 18
Christianity, 2, 18
Christianity in the 2nd century, 13
Christian mysticism, 36
Christian pilgrimage, 66
Christian prayer, 65
Christina McKenna, 10
Church Triumphant, 4
Clara Germana Cele, 9
Classical Tibetan, 45, 46
Clergy, 13
Clinical depression, 52
Collin de Plancy, 56
Colonial America, 51
Confession of faith, 20
Confession (religion), 17, 31
Confessor, 56
Contortion, 49
Convent, 52, 56
Convulsion, 65
Cottage City, Maryland, 9
Council of Carthage (398), 27
Crossway Books, 36
Crucifix, 53, 66
Crucifixion, 49
Cyril of Jerusalem, 28

Dagon, 49

Dalai Lama, 45, 47
Dallas, 21
David M. Kiely, 10
De:Adolf Rodewyk, 76
Deal with the Devil, 54, 59
Dehydration, 65
Delirium, 51
Deliverance ministry, 16, 22, 27
Demon, 1, 49, 52, 58
Demonic possession, 1, 3, 7, 8, 13, 27, 31, 49, 52, 53, 56, 62, 65, 66, 71
Demon possession, 18, 19
Demons, 21, 53
Devil, 29, 49, 56, 62, 63
Diocese, 16
Disciple (Christianity), 14
Disease, 18
Disembowelment, 49
Dissociative identity disorder, 7
Dogma, 17, 50
Dorje Shugden, 45, 47
Dorje Shugden controversy, 47
Doubleday (publisher), 36
DSM-5, 7
Duchess dAiguillon, 62

Early Christianity, 13
Eastern Orthodox Church, 18
Eating disorder, 9
Ecclesiastical, 29
Edward Hughes (exorcist), 9
Edwin Hamilton Gifford, 75
Emaciation, 64
Encyclopædia Britannica Eleventh Edition, 11
Encyclopedia of Pseudoscience, 11
England, 51
English Reformation, 29
Epilepsy, 7, 51
Episcopal Church in the United States of America, 16
Erich Schmidt-Leichner, 68
Ethiopian Orthodox Tewahedo Church, 21
Eucharist, 30
Euchologion, 18
European colonization of the Americas, 56
Eusebius, 28
Evangelical Christians, 16
Evil, 3, 13
Evil eye, 39
Execution, 54
Execution by burning, 52, 54, 61
Exhumation, 68
Exorcising the blind and mute man, 25
Exorcism, **1**, 11, 13, 27, 31, 37, 50, 53, 58, 59, 72
Exorcism at the Synagogue in Capernaum, 24

Exorcism in Christianity, **13**, 27, 65
Exorcism in Islam, **39**
Exorcism in the Catholic Church, **31**, 64
Exorcism of Roland Doe, 9
Exorcist, 1, 2, 13, 53
Exorcists, 15, 32
Extrasensory perception, 41
Eyvind Johnson, 63

Fashi, 7
Fasting, 20
Felicitas Goodman, 70
Field (agriculture), 18
Find a Grave, 70
First Issue, 70
Flagellation, 58
France, 51, 52, 56, 71
Francis Borgia, 4th Duke of Gandía, 1
Franciscan, 59
Francisco Goya, 1, 15, 32
Francis de Sales, 62
Francis of Assisi, 26
Frederick M. Smith, 10
Free State of Bavaria, 64
Friar, 9

Gabriele Amorth, 11, 18
Garuda Purana, 5
Genuflection, 67
George Lukins, 9
Georgetown University, 9
Gerasenes demonic, 24
German people, 36
Germans, 64
Gesture, 2, 13
Ghosts, 45
Ghosts in Tibetan culture, **45**
Giotto, 26
Girolamo Menghi, 11
Glossolalia, 21, 49, 58
God, 4
God in Christianity, 2, 13
Golestan Palace, 43
Gordon Stein, 10, 73
Gospel, 3, 17, 35
Gospel of John, 55
Grace (Christianity), 2, 13, 29
Greek language, 1, 59
Gustav Dore, 2, 14
Guthuk, 7, 47

Hadith, 6, 42
Hallucination, 58, 65
Hamburg State Opera, 63
Hanging, 62
Hanuman, 4, 5

Hanuman Chalisa, 5
HarperSanFrancisco, 36
Heresy, 50
Hindus, 5
Hippolytus of Rome, 28
Hoax, 60
Holy Communion, 21
Holy Name of Jesus, 4
Holy Saturday, 29
Holy See, 33
Holy Spirit, 29
Holy Trinity, 19
Holy water, 5, 21, 62
Holy well, 66
Huguenot, 63
Hungry ghost, 45
Hysteria, 7, 50, 55, 59

Ibn Qayyim al-Jawziyya, 6, 42
Ibn Taymiyyah, 39
Icon, 2, 4, 13
Infant baptism, 29
Inquisitor, 50, 53, 60
Insufflation, 15, 19
International Association of Exorcists, 29
International Crisis Group, 42
International Standard Book Number, 10, 11, 27, 64, 70, 72
International Statistical Classification of Diseases and Related Health Problems, 7
Islam, 39
Islamic scholar, 6, 42
Islamist, 42
Ittar, 5

Jean-Joseph Surin, 59
Jesuit, 8, 9, 59
Jesus, 2, 30
Jesus Christ, 3, 14, 18
Jesus exorcising a mute, 2, 14
Jesus in Christianity, 13
Jewish Encyclopedia, 14
Jinn, 6, 39
Johann Blumhardt, 9
John Lydon, 70
John Whiting, 63
Josef Stangl, 67
Josephine McCarthy, 11
Josephus, 6
Journalist, 36
Judas Iscariot, 68
Jules Michelet, 52

Kabbalah, 6
Kazuhiro Tajima-Pozo, 11
Ken Russell, 63

Kīla (Buddhism), 46
Kirtan, 5
Klingenberg am Main, 64
Krzysztof Penderecki, 63

Latin, 17, 31
Latin Church, 27
Layman, 15, 32
Leiblfing, 64, 65
Lent, 30
Leviathan, 59
Lhasa, 7, 47
Libel, 58
Lille, 55
Limina, 3, 17, 35
Litany of the Saints, 30
Liturgical books of the Roman Rite, 29
LiveScience, 73
Loudun, 56
Loudun possessions, 49–52, **56**, 71
Louis XIII, 62
Louviers, 49
Louviers possessions, **49**, 59
Lower Bavaria, 64
Lower Franconia, 64
Lucifer, 59, 68
Lutheran, 4, 9
Lutheran Church, 18, 19, 29, 31
Lutheran Church–Missouri Synod, 14
Luther Miles Schulze, 9

Magic (paranormal), 53, 56
Major depressive disorder, 65
Malachi Martin, 8, 11
Malleus Maleficarum, 61
Malnutrition, 64, 65
Mania, 7, 54
Manslaughter, 68
Mantra, 5
Marseilles, 52
Martha Broissier, 8, 62
Martha Brossier, 10, **71**, 72
Martin Luther, 15, 19
Mass (Catholic Church), 65
Matt Baglio, 36
Medical doctor, 9
Mediumship, 14
Mennonite, 20
Mercenary, 63
Messiah, 14
Michael Taylor (demoniac), 9
Michael W. Cuneo, 11
Minister (Christianity), 20, 21
Minor exorcism, 4
Minor exorcism in Christianity, **27**
Minor orders, 27

Minyan, 6
Monier Monier-Williams, 10
Monk, 62
Monomania, 8
Montague Summers, 52
Mood stabilizer, 66
Mother Teresa, 10
M. Scott Peck, 8, 11
Multiple personality disorder, 70
Music therapy, 41
Mystagogical Catechesis, 28

Names and titles of Jesus in the New Testament, 14
Narasimha, 5
Negligent homicide, 65, 68
Nero, 68
Nirvana, 45
Normandy, France, 49
Nun, 52, 56

Of Exorcisms and Certain Supplications, 17, 31
Oil of catechumens, 30
Order of Friars Minor Capuchin, 58
Order of Saint Benedict, 15, 32
Our Father, 4

Paranormal, 1
Paraphilia, 53
Parish, 56
Parlement, 61
Penance, 58
Pendle witches, 56
Penitence, 20
Pennsylvania Dutch, 20
Pentecostal Church, 22
Periciazine, 65
Peter Hall (director), 63
Pew Research Center, 21
Phantom pregnancy, 59
Phenytoin, 65
Philip of Agira, 3, 17, 35
Physician, 16, 51
Placebo, 8
Pneumonia, 67
Poitiers, 60
Poitou, 56
Pope Benedict XVI, 70
Pope Cornelius, 27
Pope Fabian, 27
Pope John Paul II, 70
Potala Palace, 7, 47
Pow-wow (folk magic), 20
Prayer, 3, 51, 54
Prelate, 32
Priest, 3, 8, 52, 56

Priesthood (Catholic Church), 21
Priests, 16
Probation, 65
Professional ethics, 8
Protestant Reformation, 15, 19
Psalm 91, 6
Psychiatrist, 9, 16
Psychiatry, 7
Psychologist, 51
Psychosis, 7, 65
Psychosurgery, 8
Psychotherapy, 8
Public domain, 31
Public Image Ltd, 70
Puja (Hinduism), 5
Purana, 5

Qalb, 39
Quran, 5, 40, 41

Rabbi, 6
Relic, 51, 71
Requiem (2006 film), 9, 36, 70
Richard Noll, 73
Rite of Christian Initiation of Adults, 30
Ritual, 1
Rituale Romanum, 3, 35
Roland Doe, 36
Roman Catholic, 8
Roman Catholic Diocese of Angers, 71
Roman Catholic Diocese of Orléans, 71
Roman Catholicism, 29
Roman Missal, 28
Roman Pontifical, 28
Roman Ritual, 18, 32, 67
Romorantin-Lanthenay, 71
Rouen, 50
Royal Shakespeare Company, 63
Rubrics, 3

Sabbath (witchcraft), 49
Sacrament, 29, 51
Sacramental, 31
Sacramentals, 4, 17
Sacraments of the Catholic Church, 17, 31
Sacrilege, 18, 32
Sahih al-Bukhari, 6, 42
Saint, 62
Saint Francis Borgia, 15, 32
Saint Padre Pio, 36
Salem witch trials, 56
Salvador Dalí, 9
San Giorgio Piacentino, 66
Sanskrit, 45, 46
Sarum Rite, 29
Satan, 27, 39, 50, 60

Satanism, 53
Satanism and Witchcraft, 52
Satire, 58
Saul, 13
Schizophrenia, 7, 65
Scrutiny, 30
Sebastien Michaelis, 53
Second Vatican Council, 29
Seizure, 51, 65
Servant Publications, 36
Sex Pistols, 70
Shakti, 5
Sheikh, 5
Shirk (Islam), 42
Shiva, 5
Shofar, 6
Shri Hanuman Mandir, Sarangpur, 4
Sicily, 3, 17, 35
Sign of the cross, 29
Sins, 20
Skeptoid podcast, 70
Society of Jesus, 69
Southern Baptist Theological Seminary, 16
Spinello Aretino, 34
Spirit, 51
Spiritual entities, 1
Standard German, 64
Starvation, 64
Statuta Ecclesiæ Antiqua, 27
St Benedict, 34
St. Cyril of Jerusalem, 15, 18
Strafgesetzbuch, 68
Strangling, 54
Strappado, 54
Suggestion, 8
Suicide, 54
Sura, 6, 41
Surat al-Falaq, 6, 41
Surat al-Ikhlas, 6, 41
Surat an-Nas, 6, 41
S:Urbain Grandier, Celebrated Crimes, 64
Symbol, 2, 13

Tanacu exorcism, 10
Tantra, 5
Taoism, 7
Template:Catholic Encyclopedia, 31
Template:Paranormal, 1
Template talk:Paranormal, 1
Temporal lobe epilepsy, 65
The Canaanite womans daughter, 23
The Devils (film), 63
The Devils of Loudun, 63
The Devils of Loudun (opera), 63
The Devils (play), 63
The Exorcism of Emily Rose, 9, 36, 65, 70

85

The Exorcist, 36
The Exorcist (novel), 9
The Guardian, 73
The New York Times, 76
Theology, 50
Theophilus Riesinger, 36
The Rite (2011 film), 36
The Rite: The Making of a Modern Exorcist, 36
The Washington Post, 69
Tibetan Buddhist, 45
Torture, 50, 54, 61
Tourettes syndrome, 7
Treatise on the Apparitions of Spirits and on Vampires or Revenants, 10, 72
Trepanation, 8
Trinity, 2, 13
True cross, 71
Tulpa, 46

United Methodist Church, 31
United States, 33
University of Würzburg, 65
Unsupported attributions, 62
Urbain Grandier, 52, 55–57, 63
Ursulines, 52, 56

Vade retro satana, 15, 33
Vajrayana, 46
Vedas, 5
Vedic, 5
Ventriloquism, 72
Vicar, 49
Virgil, 71
Vishnu, 5

Wainuiomata, 10
Wainuiomata mākutu lifting, 10
Walter F. Williams, 11
Walter Halloran, 9
Wellington, 10
Western Christianity, 27
Western Shugden Society, 47
West Germany, 64, 65
Wikipedia:Citation needed, 5, 6, 39, 41, 42, 60, 62, 63
Wikipedia:Verifiability, 41
Wiktionary:energumen, 27
William Peter Blatty, 9
William S. Bowdern, 9
William Trethowan, 11
Witchcraft, 52, 56, 58
Witches mark, 54, 60
Witch-hunt, 51, 52
WP:NOTRS, 39, 40

Xenoglossia, 59
Xenoglossy, 34

Yajna, 5
Yajur Veda, 5

Zamzam Well, 5
Zebulun, 58

www.ingramcontent.com/pod-product-compliance
Lightning Source LLC
Chambersburg PA
CBHW051348040426
42453CB00007B/474